LENIN'S LEGACY

LENIN'S LEGACY

A CONCISE HISTORY AND GUIDE TO SOVIET COLLECTIBLES

MARTIN J. GOODMAN

Schiffer Military History
Atglen, PA

Acknowledgements

I would like to thank the following people for the knowledge that I have gained over the many years and in helping me acquire the Soviet artifacts contained within this book: Serguei Tsapenko, Marion Furlan, Yuri Altshuler, Igor Moiseyev, Nat Sherbin, Alex Brokhman, Slava Olchevski, Richard Whitelaw, Dave Stuart, Frank Grant, Eli Zagov, Adam Livingstone, Louie Levstik and many others too numerous to mention. Without their friendship this book would not have been possible.

Also, a special thanks goes to Raphael and Raya Anshilevich for the many hours of work spent in helping with the Russian to English translation of the many articles herein.

I would also like to thank Robert Biondi who showed an interest and chose this project, and turned what was once a dream into reality.

Dedication
I would like to dedicate this book to my beautiful wife Shelley, and my two wonderful children Adrienne and Jamie. Thanks for your patience and support.

Photography and book design by Robert Biondi.

Copyright © 2000 by Martin J. Goodman.
Library of Congress Catalog Number: 99-66920.

Printed in China.
ISBN: 0-7643-1019-4

We are interested in hearing from authors with book ideas on military topics.

Published by Schiffer Publishing Ltd.
4880 Lower Valley Road
Atglen, PA 19310 USA
Phone: (610) 593-1777
FAX: (610) 593-2002
E-mail: Schifferbk@aol.com.
Visit our web site at: www.schifferbooks.com
Please write for a free catalog.
This book may be purchased from the publisher.
Please include $3.95 postage.
Try your bookstore first.

In Europe, Schiffer books are distributed by:
Bushwood Books
6 Marksbury Ave.
Kew Gardens
Surrey TW9 4JF
England
Phone: 44 (0)208 392-8585
FAX: 44 (0)208 392-9876
E-mail: Bushwd@aol.com.
Free postage in the UK. Europe: air mail at cost.
Try your bookstore first.

CONTENTS

INTRODUCTION

The USSR existed for seventy-four years (1917-1991) and was a superpower that had a remarkable influence throughout the world in the twentieth century.

The purpose of this book is to present a concise history of the Soviet Union with a comprehensive collection of Soviet artifacts. The symbolism presented through this collection visually enhances the scope of the USSR's great history. Each artifact within the collection has a history all its own and as the saying goes, "a picture is worth a thousand words."

The Soviet collection presented covers a wide range of topics and the artifacts herein, in essence, describes the Soviet Union itself. In the first chapter on the formation of the USSR, there are many pins and badges that were made to commemorate the October Revolution and the birth of the USSR itself. In the next chapter, a biography of Lenin is accompanied by a variety of busts and statues that were all over the country in state institutions, factories and in the military to revere the nation's founder. There is also a large collection of Lenin pins, which were worn by Soviet citizens to show their allegiance to the Communist Party. The next chapter looks at the Communist Party and the nation's government, showing badges worn by the delegates at plenums and at the Party Congresses. The Soviet security forces had an immeasurable impact on the USSR itself and on foreign countries throughout the world. In this chapter many of the badges that were worn by uniformed officers are shown. In the chapter about communism and Soviet labour it becomes apparent that awards for labour excellence, achievement and valour were an important part of the Soviet communist economy, which was unique when compared to the economies of the West. Communist youth organizations throughout the USSR were important in establishing good com-

munist foundations for Soviet youth. Of course the USSR's technical achievements in military advancement, aviation and cosmonautics, were key to its sphere of influence around the world and also provided the necessary propaganda to achieve its goals internationally. Many badges worn by Soviet military personnel are shown as well as other commemorative symbols which reflect the USSR's technical achievements throughout the decades.

I grew-up during the pinnacle of the USSR, the Brezhnev era. I remember it was very rare to find a political or military artifact from the Soviet Union at that time. Many of its symbols were considered 'national treasures' and were forbidden to leave the country. If a Soviet citizen tried to smuggle an item out of the country it could result in severe punishment or imprisonment.

During the period of 'glasnost' (openness) during the Gorbachev era in the late 1980s, artifacts started to leave slowly to the West. After the collapse of the Soviet Union in December 1991, the symbolism itself was not required anymore and even greater numbers of artifacts started leaving the country to the West eventually for collectors to buy. The unfortunate Russian people of which approximately eighty percent are living in poverty have resorted to selling their 'national treasures' in the form of orders, medals, badges, etc., for hard currency and American dollars. Employees in government offices, institutions, factories, military servicemen, and sailors on navy ships, would pilfer the 'national treasures' and sell them on the 'black market'. Soviet surplus items that were still in the warehouses would be sold for badly needed money as they were not needed any more.

It has been said that in the late 1990s, Boris Yeltsin and the Russian government wanted to put a stop to the outflow of these former 'national treasures' from continually leaving the country. But customs officers receiving the appropriate bribes, still let the items leave the country for obvious reasons.

This book covers a wide variety of topics in its discussion of the history of the USSR and is designed to be a comprehensive guide for collectors, while also providing a background history to enhance the collecting experience. It is also intended for all those interested in the history of the USSR and interested in its symbolism, which is shown through the artifacts revealed herein. These artifacts were once forbidden to leave the country and consequently were not seen by many of us in the West when the USSR was a superpower.

The Soviet Union does not exist anymore, but there are many socialist countries and many capitalist countries that still use socialist principles in their governments. Vladimir Lenin and the resultant birth of socialism had a profound influence on the twentieth century and 'Lenin's Legacy' still remains.

ONE

THE FORMATION OF THE USSR

During the latter part of the Nineteenth century the majority of the Russian people had to endure a very hard life. As a result of the difficult social-economic conditions that existed in Russia at that time, the world's first socialist state the Union of Soviet Socialist Republics (USSR) was created. It was by no means an accident, as there were two major social-economic factors that led to its creation.

The first contributing factor was the existence of the monarchy in Russia. The first ruler to be called 'czar' was Ivan the Terrible in the year 1547. Ivan the Terrible and the czars that followed him passed laws that bound the peasants to the land as serfs. Feudalism was the economic, political, and social structure in Russian at that time. During the next few hundred years under czarist rule, the serfs lived in bondage as slaves to the nobility which were the landowners.

As a consequence of the discontentment of the Russian people Czar Alexander II in 1861 created the Emancipation Statute, which was a series of political and social reforms to strengthen the economy and improve the life of the Russian people and especially the peasants. One of the most notable reforms of the statute was to free the serfs from their masters, the nobility and allow them to purchase land for themselves. It was however unsuccessful, as few peasants had enough money to buy the land that they required to make a comfortable living for their families. If they did manage to buy the land, they then were required to pay stiff redemption payments to the government, which ultimately was used as compensation for their former landowners. The Emancipation Statute was a great disappointment and actually created a growing discontentment among the peasantry.

At the other end of the spectrum, the end of serfdom caused a decline in the status of the nobility and as a result of this, some of the nobility eventually joined the growing revolutionary force that was developing in Russia at that time.

The second contributing factor was the modernization of Russia, which was a result of the industrial revolution of the 1800s. During the late 1800s, Russia's industrialization grew rapidly. New industries were created and Russia's working class grew substantially during this period. Workers lived in ghettos located on the outskirts of the cities. The living conditions in the worker's districts were horrible. There was overcrowding as two or three families lived in one apartment. The sanitation was poor and to make matters worse, the unpaved roads in the ghettos often turned into mud compounding the misery. To add to the burden, the worker's wages were extremely low so they could barely afford the necessities of life.

Not only were the living conditions dreadful but the conditions in the factories were difficult as well. Factory workers often worked twelve-hour days and only had Sundays off. In the factories working conditions were extremely unsafe and unhealthy, as there was no legislation to protect the workers. It was as if the Russian worker was literally working himself to death due to the abhorrent conditions in the factories. Workers were treated like slaves and had no dignity. The employers ruled their factories as the czar ruled the country. It was the Russian worker who would eventually play a leading role in the coming revolution.

Due to the hardships the citizens of Russia had to endure, a revolutionary movement developed during the latter part of the 1800s. The revolutionary goal was to bring down the autocracy and create a more just society for the ordinary people.

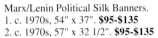

Marx/Lenin Political Silk Banners.
1. c. 1970s, 54" x 37". **$95-$135**
2. c. 1970s, 57" x 32 1/2". **$95-$135**

Slogans on front -
Top left: Workers of All Countries, Unite!
Bottom: Under the Banner of Marxism-Leninism,
Under the Leadership of the Communist Party – Forward, to the Victory of
Communism!
Text on back: Glory Union of Soviet Socialist Republics!

In 1869, two revolutionaries Sergei Nachaev and Michael Bakunin prepared an article called 'The Catechism of the Revolutionary', which had two profound statements in it worth mentioning. The article stated that the revolutionary is an individual who has severed all its ties with society and "continues to inhabit it with only one purpose – destroy it." The Catechism also stated that everything which, "promotes the success of the revolution is moral, everything that hinders it is immoral." These profound statements which indicated the use of centralized terror had a great influence on many of the Russian revolutionaries at that time. A more moderate approach was adopted by the Populist revolutionaries. They were young men and women which were members of the intelligentsia. They promoted the use of organized education of the masses to cause the revolutionary change in Russian society. In 1873, thousands of the young intelligentsia left the cities and went into the Russian villages to educate the peasants about their revolutionary message. The results of the campaign were unsuccessful. The uneducated and backward peasantry could not understand the context of their message and ultimately accepted the continued existence of the czardom. The rural peasantry also had an inherent mistrust towards the young intelligentsia that were from the big cities. The czarist police intervened and hindered the success of the campaign as well.

As a consequence of the dismal failure of the young intelligentsia's campaign, the use of centralized terror became the policy for the revolutionary movement. The People's Will was the name of this new terrorist organization. One of the most notable events occurred in 1887, when a plot to kill Czar Alexander III was discovered and the czarist police arrested the revolutionaries involved. One of the revolutionaries who was detained was Alexander Ulyanov who said, "There is no better way of dying than to lay down one's life for one's country. Such a death does not fill honest and sincere men with fear. I have had but one aim: to serve the unfortunate Russian people." This young man who was hanged three days later was Vladimir Ulyanov's older brother by four years. Vladimir Ulyanov commonly known by his pseudonym LENIN, became known in history as the leader of the Russian revolution. Lenin's brother Alexander had a profound influence on Lenin himself and undoubtedly stirred Lenin towards revolutionary activities.

As a consequence of the Populist and People's Will failures, Marxism became the ideology of the Russian revolutionary intelligentsia in the late 1880s. Karl Marx was a German philosopher and revolutionary whose writings stated that it was the working class who would form the core of the revolutionary movement and move society towards socialism.

Russian Marxism became the doctrine of the political group called the Russian Social Democratic Labour Party (RSDLP) which was formed in 1898. Notable members of the RSDLP were Georgy Plekhanov who was a leading philosopher and revolutionary of Russian Marxism, Julius Martov who eventually became the leader of the Mensheviks, and Vladimir Ilyich Ulyanov (Lenin) who became the leader of the Bolsheviks and ultimately the leader of the Russian revolution.

In July 1903, at the Second Congress of the RSDLP, two proposals with respect to the organization of the Party were addressed. Martov proposed a Party encompassing both professional revolutionaries and those among the working and middle classes who sympathized with the Party's platform. The membership would have an influence on Party policy and could contribute to it on a part-time basis. Lenin on the other hand, wanted the Party to be composed of a small group of full-time dedicated revolutionaries that were highly disciplined, ideologically unified, which would create an organization of centralized power that would organize the working class towards revolution.

After long and heated debates at the Second Congress about the organization of the Party, some members abstained from voting, while others outright left. The result was Lenin's proposal winning by a majority of just two votes. His supporters were subsequently labeled the Bolsheviks - the 'majority', while Martov's supporters were labeled the Mensheviks - the 'minority'. In the years that followed the Bolsheviks and the Mensheviks evolved into separate political parties both advocating socialism but in a different form. The Mensheviks rejected the centralized power of the Bolsheviks. The irreconcilable split eventually would result in the Civil War that enveloped Russia for two years (1918-1920) after the Bolsheviks assumed power in 1917.

The workers couldn't take their anguish any longer and the first revolution in Russia occurred on Sunday, January 22, 1905. Father Gapon led the workers of St. Petersburg on a peaceful demonstration to the winter palace bearing a petition to the czar listing their distresses. Their petition stated, "We are impoverished and oppressed, unbearable work is imposed upon us, we are despised and not recognized as human beings. We are treated as slaves, who must bear their fate and be silent. We have suffered terrible things but we are pressed even deeper into the abyss of poverty, ignorance and lack of rights." It was a peaceful demonstration with justifiable concerns but their voices were not heard.

When the peaceful precession of marchers approached the gates of the palace the czarist police and army regiments awaited. Without warning they shot at the crowd of demonstrators leaving 800 people dead and wounded. The snow that winter's day was stained with the blood of the demonstrators and this day in history has become known as 'Bloody Sunday'. From this day onward Russia would be absorbed in a social unrest that would shake the foundations of imperialist Russia.

In October of the same year, the workers of St. Petersburg formed the Soviet of Worker's Deputies. The purpose of the Soviet of Worker's Deputies was to organize strikes and represent the workers in the factories promoting better working conditions and worker's rights. The president of its Central Committee was Leon Trotsky who would become a leading figure during the October Revolution of 1917 and during the Civil War that followed.

As a result of the continued unrest throughout the land Czar Nicholas II approved the creation of the newly elected Duma, the parliament in Russia. The capitalist bourgeois government ministers of the Duma continued to be responsible to the czar. The czar therefore, ruled the country through his ministers without regards to the elected assembly. The czar had the ultimate power to veto all resolutions adopted by the assembly of the Duma and dissolve it if necessary. The first Dumas of 1906 and 1907 were both dissolved as a consequence of the assembly being opposed to government policy. This rendered the elected assembly of the Duma essentially without power and Russia's attempt at democracy was a failure and left the people in continued despair.

There was social discontentment and unrest among the Russian people for the next twelve years as life was not improving. In August 1914, Czar Nicholas II announced Russia's entry into World War I. The czar was counting on Russian patriotism to restore the prestige of the monarchy. The bourgeoisie capitalists were in favour of the war effort as industrial production increased and profits soared, as it was utilized in supplying goods for the military. Workers did not benefit from this as wages and working conditions did not improve, and those that went on strike or opposed the government were sent to the front to fight in the war, which almost meant certain death. As a consequence of industry concentrating on the supply of goods for the war effort, there was a severe shortage of food, clothing, fuel, etc. for the population. Russia was not in a position to enter a prolonged war. Russia's infrastructure was incapable of managing the war effort. It lacked the necessary armament and the social climate within the country was also unfavourable for such an undertaking.

By the end of 1916, Russia suffered a staggering 5.5 million casualties of which over 2 million were prisoners, 3.5 million were dead or wounded. The total loss of life is estimated between 1.6 to 1.85 million people. World War I ultimately became an immense disaster for the czarist regime and the Russian economy continued to deteriorate because of it. The Russian people were now at their breaking point.

'Glory Great October' Wall Plaque. **$85-$110**
Cast aluminum, 6" diameter.

October Revolution Commemorative Pins, c. 1970s-1980s. **$5-$10**

1917 - "The Great October"

1917 was the decisive year. The first revolution of 1917 occurred early in that year. It was on March 8, International Women's Day in St. Petersburg, that thousands of women left their work at the textile mills and started protesting in the streets shouting, "bread! bread! bread!" By the afternoon there were over 50,000 demonstrators in the streets of St. Petersburg chanting, "We have nothing to eat!", "Our children are starving!", and "Down with the autocracy!", "Stop the war!"

On March 9, the second day of the protest, there was great excitement, anticipation and enthusiasm among the people of the workers' districts. More than 150,000 workers and university students took to the streets in protest.

On March 10, the third day of the protest, the protest escalated into a general strike that encompassed all sectors of the working class. The city was paralyzed and the government was in a state of siege. A turn of events occurred in favour of the demonstrators, as the Cossacks the elite cavalry units for the czar, started to show sympathy for the demonstrators and withdrew their sabers. This was a great moral booster for the demonstrators.

On March 11, the fourth day of the protest, czarist police and soldiers were called to counter the unrest in the city. During that day, crowds of demonstrators converged at the center of the city. Exactly twelve years ago to that winter, history repeated itself again. Without warning the czarist police and soldiers shot at the crowds leaving 300 dead and wounded. The snow that winter's day was stained again with the blood of the demonstrators as it was on the 'Bloody Sunday' of 1905.

On March 12, the fifth day of the protest, an unprecedented event occurred that shifted the tide of the revolution. An armed insurrection against the government was underway, which was led by 25,000 soldiers that joined the demonstrators. By the time evening rolled around almost the entire Petrograd garrison had gone on the side of the working people, which effectively gave the revolutionaries control of the entire city.

On March 13, the revolution came to a climax. The last remaining soldiers loyal to the czar surrendered or fled the city. The insurgents began arresting the ministers, generals, and police officers of the czarist regime. A provisional government was formed and new cabinet ministers were appointed to the Duma. The Provisional Government's leaders were not elected by the people but were liberals who previously had seats in the Duma. During the previous day, the militant workers and socialist party leaders reestablished the Petrograd Soviet, which was first established during the 1905 revolution. The Petrograd Soviet was given a new name, The Soviet of Workers' and Soldiers' Deputies, as elected representatives from the factories and soldiers from the army garrisons would sit together in the Petrograd Soviet. As a consequence of these six days of revolution Russia now had two political centers of power, the Provisional Government and The Soviet of Workers' and Soldiers' Deputies.

On March 14, 1917, the czarist regime had collapsed and Czar Nicholas II abdicated the throne and Imperial Russia existed no more.

Russia was now being governed by two independent governments. The Provisional Government represented the upper classes and liberal reformers, while the Soviet of Workers' and Soldiers' Deputies represented the working class and the soldiers. An obvious rivalry existed between the two sides and this would continue until October of that year.

This time in Russian history is known as 'The Dual Power'. On April 22, 1917, Lenin wrote an article in Pravda the Bolshevik newspaper. He wrote about the 'The Dual Power' and stated: "Along side the Provisional Government, the government of the bourgeoisie, another government has risen, so far weak and incipient, but undoubtedly a government that actually exists and is growing – the Soviets of Workers' and Soldiers' Deputies."

"What is the class composition of this other government? It consists of the proletariat and the peasants in soldiers' uniforms. What is the political nature of this government? it is a revolutionary dictatorship, i.e., a power directly based on revolutionary seizure, on the direct initiative of the people from below, and not on a law enacted by a centralized State power."

Between March and October of that year, concessions were made between the Provisional Government and the workers, as well as the peasants. Some of the concessions agreed upon were an eight hour work day and the worker's right to strike. The peasants also wanted solutions to their agrarian problems such as ownership of land and the right to sell their produce. The Provisional Government agreed to have the Constituent Assembly meet as soon as possible to address the agrarian concern of the peasants.

For revolutionary times however, the concessions fell short of meeting the demands of the workers and the peasants. The worker's demands of better working conditions and higher wages were ignored and the peasant's demands for the ownership of land were also ignored.

As a result of the February revolution, thousands of veteran revolutionaries who were detained under czarist persecution were released from Siberian exile or prison. Some of them returned from foreign countries where they were hiding. Released from Siberian exile were such notable Bolsheviks as Yakov Sverdlov, the first Chairman of the All-Russian Central Executive Committee, Lev Kamenev, the Chairman of the Moscow Soviet and member of the Politburo, Joseph Djugashvili, better known as Stalin, who became the next leader of the Communist Party after Lenin. From a Moscow prison came Felix Dzerzhinskii, who became the head of the 'Cheka' the Soviet secret police. From North America came Lev Davidovich Bronstein, better known as Trotsky, who was the President of the Petrograd Soviet and who became the Commissar of War and first Chief of the Red Army. From Switzerland via Germany in a 'sealed train' came thirty-eight exiles. Among them was Grigory Zinoviev, who would become the Chairman of the Petrograd Soviet and the Comintern and a member of the Politburo. Accompanying him was Vladimir Lenin, the leader of the Bolshevik faction of the Russian Social Democratic Labour Party (RSDLP) and ultimately the first leader of the Communist Party of the Soviet Union (CPSU).

On April 16, 1917, Lenin via the 'sealed train' arrived at Finland Station in Petrograd. The Bolsheviks had arranged a great reception for him as thousands of workers and soldiers greeted him waving red flags and banners. During this month Lenin wrote his famous 'The April Theses'. In it he wrote, "It must be explained to the masses that the Soviet of Worker's Deputies is the only possible form of revolutionary government and, therefore, our task is, while the government is submitting to the influence of the bourgeoisie, to present a patient, systematic, and persistent analysis of its errors and tactics, an analysis especially adapted to the practical needs of the masses."

"While we are in the minority, we carry on the work of criticism and of exposing errors, advocating all along the necessity of transferring the entire power of states to the Soviets of Workers' Deputies, so that the masses might learn from experience how to rid themselves of errors." He stated that the Provisional Government did not represent the interests of the Russian people and all power should be immediately transferred to the Soviets.

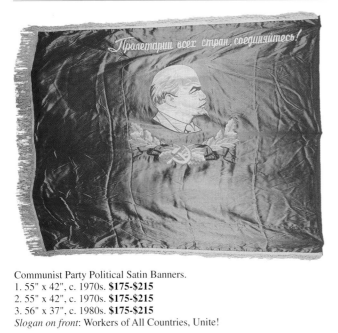

Communist Party Political Satin Banners.
1. 55" x 42", c. 1970s. **$175-$215**
2. 55" x 42", c. 1970s. **$175-$215**
3. 56" x 37", c. 1980s. **$175-$215**
Slogan on front: Workers of All Countries, Unite!

The Bolshevik Central Committee initially found his theses too radical and rejected it with an overwhelming majority. Lenin with his intelligence and great persuasive abilities was eventually able to persuade the Bolshevik Party to follow his programme.

By the end of May 1917, the Bolsheviks organized factory committees which were designed to replace the moderate trade unions. The factory committees organized the worker's militia into the Red Guard, which would be an important force for the Bolsheviks in the coming October.

By the middle of the year, discontentment continued to grow among the people against the Provisional Government. Russia's participation in World War I created severe hardships for the country and its people. There were shortages of food, fuel and clothing. The war became a major issue for the government. The middle and upper classes stayed loyal to the allies and supported the war effort as they still agreed with the former policies of the czar. While the workers and soldiers opposed the war as it was killing millions of their people and destroying the economy.

The Soviet of Workers' and Soldiers' Deputies was comprised of left-wing socialist parties of which the Bolsheviks were one of the many. The Bolsheviks at this time were a minority within the Soviet. It was the Bolshevik faction of the Soviet of Workers' and Soldiers' Deputies that absolutely refused to collaborate with the Provisional Government and was politically untainted by the war and the failures of the country's economy. The Bolshevik Party offered a distinct alternative to the Provisional Government. They wanted an immediate end to the war and the elimination of the Provisional Government. Bolshevik slogans started to appear at demonstrations, "Peace! Land! Bread!" and "All Power to the Soviets."

During the 'July Days', demonstrations by workers and soldiers occurred in the capital. Many of the protesters looked to the Bolsheviks for leadership. The Bolsheviks decided not to attempt an insurrection at that time because they did not have enough support from the peasants in rural Russia and from the citizens throughout Russia in general. They did not have enough overall support at that time and if they did assume power, it would have been very fragile and may not have lasted.

During the remaining months of the year the Bolshevik slogans of "Peace! Land! Bread!" and "All Power to the Soviets" clearly stated the platform of the Party and was welcomed by the desperate people of Russia. The Bolsheviks wanted an immediate end to the war, supported land being transferred to the peasants and an immediate transfer of power to the Sovi-

Left: All Power to the Soviets Pin, c. 1970s. **$5-$10**
Right: Land for the Peasants Pin, c. 1970s. **$5-$10**

ets. The Mensheviks and the Social Revolutionaries, instead of assuming power, were more pre-occupied with siding with the Provisional Government and the bourgeoise, promoting the new democracy instead of defending the concerns of the working class and the peasants. The working class and the peasants subsequently turned to the Bolsheviks for leadership. By September the Bolsheviks had won majorities in the Moscow and Petrograd Soviets and made great gains in the regional Soviets as well. The moderate socialist Parties were slowly losing ground as their membership was shrinking. The campaign created an explosion in the Bolshevik Party membership as it grew from 60,000 to nearly 250,000 by October.

Alexander Kerensky the Prime Minister of the Provisional Government insisted on Russia's continuance in the war. The war effort was clearly beyond Russia's capacity at that time and already had resulted in millions of casualties. During the second week of October, Kerensky wanted to send the Petrograd garrison to the war front. The entire Petrograd garrison refused and called for an immediate transfer of power to the Soviets and pledged their complete support to the Bolshevik dominated Soviet.

The Soviet formed a new defense organization called the Military Revolutionary Committee of the Petrograd Soviet under the leadership of Trotsky. On November 5 at the House of the People, Trotsky appealed to an enthusiastic crowd, "to support the Soviet that has taken on itself the glorious burden of bringing the victory of the revolution to a conclusion, and of giving peace, land, and bread!"

The support for the Provisional Government was very weak and the Bolsheviks were debating if this was the time for an insurrection. On the afternoon of November 6 (October 24 old calendar), sailors of the battle cruiser Aurora refused orders from their superiors to put the ship to sea and offered their full support to the Bolsheviks. Later that evening Lenin arrived at the Bolshevik Party headquarters at the Smolny Institute. Lenin was furious at the hesitation exhibited by the Central Committee of the Party in moving the revolution forward. Lenin became the impetus that would push the Party forward to make preparations for the insurrection.

On the infamous day of November 7 (October 25 old calendar), the day that was scheduled for the Congress of Soviets in Petrograd, the revolution began. In the early morning hours at 2:00 am the armed workers known as Red Guards, the Petrograd garrison and the revolutionary sailors, on orders from the Military Revolutionary Committee of the Petrograd Soviet, seized the post offices, telephone buildings, state bank, railroad stations, bridges, and the main power station shutting off all electricity to the government buildings.

It was just after 9:30 pm that fateful day, that the sailors on the cruiser Aurora anchored nearby in the Neva River started firing their shells signaling the siege of the Winter Palace. Thousands of Red Guards and sailors stormed the Winter Palace. With little resistance the Bolshevik forces occupied the Winter Palace the house of the Provisional Government. The Provisional Government fell and was no more.

The Second Congress of Soviets convened at 10:30 pm that evening in the great white ballroom of the Smolny Institute the Bolshevik headquarters. The Mensheviks and the other moderate socialist parties denounced the actions of the Bolsheviks, as they felt the government would be made up exclusively of Bolshevik representatives. The moderates wanted an elected government made up of a broad coalition of socialist representatives.

Also during the Second Congress of Soviets members of the new Soviet government were announced and Lenin became Chairman of the Council of People's Commissars (Sovnarkom). Amidst the cheers and adulation Lenin entered the hall and stood at the podium proclaiming, "We will now proceed to construct the socialist order."

Lenin also stated the decrees of the new Soviet government, 1. Peace - end Russia's involvement in the devastating war, 2. Land - all lands belonging to the landlords would be transferred to the peasants, 3. Dictatorship of the Proletariat - workers control of the factories.

The Soviet period in Russian history had begun and the world's first socialist State was born.

10th Year of the October Revolution Badge, c. 1927. **$165-$185**

30th Year of the October Revolution Badges, c. 1947. **$55-$85**

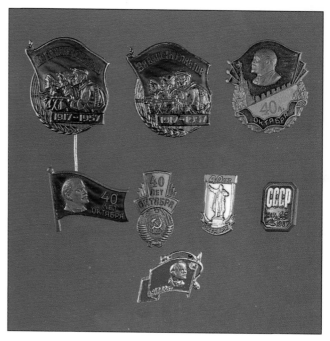

40th Year of the October Revolution Badges, c. 1957. **$45-$65**

50th Year of the October Revolution 1917-1967, Lenin Bronze Table Medallion. c. 1967. **$80-$95**
Text on back: With Your, Comrade (Lenin), Heart and Name (Soul) We Think, Breathe, Fight, and Live!

Coins Commemorating the 50th Year of the October Revolution, coins issued 1967.
1. 20 Kopeck, Fifty Years of Soviet Power 1917-1967. **$10-$15**
2. One Ruble, Fifty Years of Soviet Power (Proof). **$45-$55**

Order of the October Revolution. **$200-$250**
Awarded for the building and defence of Soviet power, governmental activities and for contributions in the economy, science and culture. Instituted October 31, 1967 for the 50th Anniversary of the October Revolution and over 100,000 were issued.

50th Year of the October Revolution Pins, c. 1967. **$5-$10**

60th Year of the October Revolution 1917-1977 Table Medallion, c. 1977.
$80-$95
Text on front: Lenin's Path!
Text on back: 60th Year of the Great October Socialist Revolution.

One Ruble Coin Commemorating the 60th Year of the October Revolution
1917-1977, coin issued 1977. **$10-$15**

70th Year of the October Revolution 1917-1987 Table Medallion, c. 1987.
$80-$95
Text on back: 70th Year of the Great October Socialist Revolution.

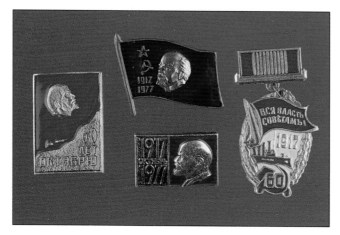

60th Year of the October Revolution Pins, c. 1977. **$5-$10**

Right: Coins Commemorating the 70th Year of the Great October Socialist
Revolution, coins issued 1987.
1. 1 Ruble (Proof). **$20-$25**
2. 3 Rubles (Proof). **$25-$35**
3. 5 Rubles (Proof). **$45-$55**

70th Year of the October Revolution Pins, c. 1987. **$5-$10**

TWO

LENIN

The focal point of this book is centered around the founder of the Soviet Union, Vladimir Ilyich Ulyanov, commonly known as LENIN. He was born on April 22, 1870, in the town of Simbirsk, now called Ulyanovsk on the Volga River. It was in 1901, that Vladimir Ilyich adopted the pseudonym Lenin, as many revolutionaries changed their names in order to make it difficult for the czarist police to identify them.

Lenin had two brothers and three sisters. It was his brother Alexander, who was four years older, who had a great influence on his life. In 1887, Alexander was a member of the revolutionary movement in Russia. On May 20, 1887, he was hanged for taking part in an assassination attempt on Czar Alexander III. At his trial Alexander said he wanted to kill the czar, "To serve the unfortunate Russian people." This tragedy deeply affected Lenin as he eventually joined the revolutionary movement while he was in university as his brother did previously.

In December 1887, while taking part in revolutionary activities while studying at the Kazan University Lenin was expelled. It was during the winter of 1888, that Lenin started studying social revolutionary literature. He studied Karl Marx's 'Das Kapital' and the book that compelled him the most was Nikolai Chernyshevsky's 'What is to be done', which he read over and over. In Chernyshevsky's book Lenin learned much and said, "Any correctly thinking and truly honest person must be a revolutionary, but also something more important: what a revolutionary should be like, what rules he should follow, how he should approach his goal and what means and methods he should use to achieve it." In 1889, Lenin translated Marx's 'The Communist Manifesto' into Russian. He was eventually permitted to study law through external studies with the St. Petersburg University. In 1891, Lenin graduated with his law degree with top marks.

By 1893, Lenin was absorbed in the study of Marxism and he had joined many Marxist circles. Lenin the revolutionary now considered himself a Marxist. In February 1894 while Lenin was in St. Petersburg, he joined a Marxist circle and would meet his future wife Nadezhda Krupskaya who he would marry within the next four years. In May 1895, Lenin traveled to Europe for the first time to make acquaintances with other Marxists. He met Georgy Plekhanov the leading philosopher and revolutionary of Russian Marxism.

In September 1895, Lenin returned to St. Petersburg and was working for the Union of Struggle for the Liberation of the Working Class where he met Julius Martov, the future leader of the Mensheviks. At a meeting on the night of December 8, Lenin and other members of the St. Petersburg Marxists were arrested for preparing the illegal newspaper 'The Worker's Cause'. He was imprisoned in jail for fifteen months and on February 1897, Lenin was submitted to Siberian exile for three years. During the same time period Krupskaya his fiancee was also exiled to Siberia. They arranged with the authorities to be exiled in the same town of Shushenskoe and on July 22, 1898 they were married.

It was on March 13-15, 1898, that the First Congress of the All-Russian Social Democratic Labour Party (RSDLP) convened. Lenin heard about this while he was in exile and declared, "From now on I am a member of the RSDLP." Unfortunately, the first Congress did not amount to much, as only nine people attended and shortly afterwards most of them were arrested. Lenin's exile ended on February 10, 1900. Those three

Photograph of Lenin One Year after the Revolution in October 1918 by P. Otsup.

Oil on Canvas Paintings of Lenin based on the photograph of Lenin in October 1918 by P. Otsup.
1. by V. Serov c. 1947, 33 1/2" x 25 1/2". **$2500-$3500**
2. c. 1950s, 43" x 34". **$2500-$3500**

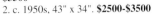

Lenin Pins of the photograph by P. Otsup, c. 1970s. **$5-$10**

Oil on Canvas Painting of Lenin c. 1940s-1950s, 33" x 25 1/4". **$2500-$3500**

Lenin – Leader Poster by V. Kononov. "Plakat" Publishers Moscow, c. 1988. **$25-$35**

22 April – The Day of the Birth of Lenin Poster by V. Sachkov. "Plakat" Publishers Moscow, c. 1987. **$25-$35** *Text on bottom*: All Over the World An Expanding Procession – of Thoughts, Words and the Causes of Ilyich.

One Ruble Coins Commemorating the Birth of Lenin.
1. One Hundred Years since the Birth of V.I. Lenin 1870-1970, coin issued 1970. **$10-$15**
2. V.I. Lenin 1870-1924, coin issued 1985. **$10-$15**

Table Medallions Commemorating 100 Years since the Birth of Lenin 1870-1970 by Myakovskii, c. 1970.
1. 1870-1970 All Over the World An Expanding Procession – of Thoughts, Words and the Causes of Ilyich Vl. Myakovskii. **$45-$55**
2. 1870-1970 Lenin Lived, Lenin Lives, Lenin Will Live! V. Myakovskii. **$35-$45**

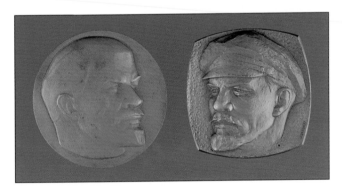 

1870-1970 Bronze Lenin Table Medallions, c. 1970.
1. 1870-1970. **$80-$95**
2. 1870 1970 by A. Korolyook. **$80-$95**

100 Lenin Bronze Table Medallion with Case by Toromonyan. **$80-$95**

1870-1970 Lenin Table Medallion, c. 1970. **$55-$65**
Text on front: One Hundred Years since the Birth of V.I. Lenin.
Text on back: Ulyanovsk . Memorial Center.

"100" Lenin Medallion. **$25-$40**

1870-1970 Lenin Desk Stand c. 1970, 2 3/4" x 2". **$55-$75**

100 Years of Lenin's Birth 1870-1970 Commemorative Pins, c. 1970. **$5-$10**

110 Years since the Birth of V.I. Lenin Table Medallion, c. 1980. **$85-$115**
Text on back: Thus We Knew Him, Thus We Remember Him, Thus He Will Live Forever.

years of exile were useful preparation for Lenin the revolutionary, as he wrote numerous articles in various Marxist newspapers.

Lenin was convinced that the future of the RSDLP depended on the establishment of a Marxist newspaper, which would be published outside of Russia away from the czarist authorities and would eventually be smuggled into Russia. After his exile, Lenin settled in Europe to join Plekhanov, Martov, Trotsky and other Marxists to create the revolutionary newspaper 'Iskra' (The Spark). Lenin wrote many articles for the paper and he did most of the editing.

It was in March 1902, that Lenin published his famous work 'What Is To Be Done?' In it he stated his concepts for the organization of the Party and wrote, "Give us an organization of revolutionaries and we shall turn Russia upside-down." In this work he clearly stated that the Party should consist of a centralized organization of full-time dedicated professional revolutionaries working to represent the working class and promote the revolution.

On July 30, 1903, the Second Congress of the All-Russian Social Democratic Labour Party (RSDLP) opened in Brussels, but due to police intervention, it was adjourned and reconvened in London on August 11. The Second Congress of the RSDLP would have a tremendous impact on the future of the socialist Party. Lenin and his followers wanted a centralized Party membership of full-time revolutionaries, trained professionals to lead the Party and would organize the working class. Martov and his followers had a more moderate approach wanting a less centralized Party not to be in total control by its leaders, allowing the individual within the membership to have more influence. Martov was working towards a broad-based Party, while Lenin's vision was a Party of a much narrower scope. Trotsky was present at the Congress and stated, "But that's dictatorship you're advocating." Lenin replied, "There is no other way." Initially Martov won the majority of the votes. But by the end of the Congress, as a result of political maneuverings and delegates walking out of the Congress, Lenin and his supporters won by a slim majority vote. They became known as the Bolsheviks (the majority), while Martov's supporters became known as the Mensheviks (the minority). The splitting of the RSDLP made Lenin the leader of the Bolsheviks.

The editorial board of 'Iskra' was made up of a majority of Mensheviks and Lenin wanted more control. He was initially successful by removing three of the Mensheviks from the editorial board leaving the board consisting of three members, Plekhanov, Martov, and himself. Martov requested that

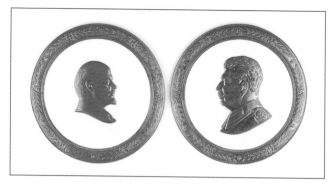

Lenin and Stalin Brass and White Enamel Wall Plaques, c. 1940s-1950s. Leningrad Mint, 5" diameter. **$130-$150**

the three removed Mensheviks should be reinstated or he would resign from the board. Plekhanov in an attempt to reunite the Party also requested that the three Menshevik members should be reinstated. Due to the quarreling, on November 1, 1903, Lenin resigned from the editorial board and 'Iskra' essentially became a Menshevik newspaper.

During the next couple of years Lenin spent most of his time writing revolutionary articles in his newly formed newspaper called 'Vperyod' (Forward) and attended many socialist meetings. He stayed in Europe as it was very difficult to carry on with revolutionary activities in Russia. After the 'Bloody Sunday' revolution in Russia, Lenin returned back to Russia in November 1905 and attended a meeting of Bolshevik functionaries, a Menshevik conference, and he also attended a session of the St. Petersburg Soviet. During this period Lenin made trips back and forth between St. Petersburg and Finland.

It was at the First All-Russian Bolshevik Conference in Finland on December 25, 1905, that Lenin met Stalin for the first time. Stalin wrote this interesting first impression, "How great was my disappointment to see that Lenin had arrived at the conference before the other delegates were there and had settled himself somewhere in a corner and was unassumingly carrying on a conversation, a most ordinary conversation, with the most ordinary delegates. I will not conceal from you that at that time this seemed to me to be rather a violation of certain essential rules." This intriguing statement by Stalin not only reveals something about Lenin, but also reveals something about the character of Stalin himself.

Lenin stayed in Europe writing many articles and attending various conferences and did not return to Russia until 1917. On June 18, 1912, the Prague Conference of the Bolsheviks had opened. It was at this conference that the Bolsheviks formed an organizationally independent Party and hence 'Bolshevism' was created. Lenin chaired the conference and the resolutions he brought forward for the Party were adopted. In the summer of 1912 in St. Petersburg the Bolsheviks establish a revolutionary newspaper of their own called 'Pravda' (Truth), which Lenin became its editor and chief contributor. The break between the Bolsheviks and the Mensheviks became irreconcilable.

The outbreak of World War I began in August 1914. Lenin was against the war as he believed the workers were fighting the war for the benefit of the capitalists. He also accepted the position that if the war would continue, a defeat would weaken the capitalist government and therefore urged the socialists "to transform the imperialist war into a Civil War." The war was devastating for the Russian people and the country as a whole. By the year 1917, there were 5.5 million Russian casualties and the Russian economy had suffered greatly. Unrest was mounting in the nation as low pay and food shortages made life miserable for the population. On March 8, 1917, was the beginning of the first revolution in Russia, as up to 200,000 workers in Petrograd in the days that followed went on a general strike. In conjunction with the revolution, the organization called the Soviet of Workers' and Soldiers' Deputies was reestablished in Petrograd. The Petrograd Soviet was initially established in 1905 after the 'Bloody Sunday' revolution to represent the working class. Due to the turmoil in the country Czar Nicholas II abdicated his thrown. The Duma, the Russian parliament, was established and it shared power with the Petrograd Soviet. This period of time became known as 'The Dual Power'. The Bolsheviks however, demanded that all power be transferred to the Soviets.

As these events were taking place in Russia, Lenin was in Zurich, Switzerland. When Lenin heard the news of the revolution he immediately started making plans for his return to Russia. Through negotiations with a Swiss socialist and the German ambassador in Switzerland, the German's agreed to have Lenin and thirty-two Russian émigrés travel through Europe to Finland in a 'sealed train'. The 'sealed train' allowed them secure travel through Europe without passport or personal checks. The German's were anxious to keep the journey of the Russian revolutionaries a secret from their own people and from the allies they were fighting. The revolutionaries also wanted the journey to be kept a secret as well, as they did not want the Russian people to believe they were collaborators with the Germans. The German government agreed to have the revolutionaries travel through Germany and ultimately to Russia, as they thought disruption of political activities in Russia would be advantageous for them in their war effort against Russia. The 'sealed train' left Switzerland on April 9, 1917.

'There Is Such A Party!' Poster of Lenin by V. Sachkov. "Plakat" Publishers Moscow, c. 1986. **$25-$35**

On April 16, 1917 at 11:00 pm the 'sealed train' arrived at Finland Station, Petrograd to an enthusiastic crowd of Bolshevik supporters. The Bolsheviks had been distributing leaflets in the city with the words "Lenin arrives today. Meet him". Amongst the cheering crowd Lenin stepped off the train onto an arrival platform and made a short speech proclaiming, "... we have to fight for a socialist revolution, to fight until the proletariat wins full victory! Long live the world socialist revolution!"

After Lenin's arrival in Petrograd, he presented his proposals on the development of the socialist revolution at various conferences and congresses in Petrograd. The famous document that Lenin wrote, which had the proposals in it, is known as Lenin's 'April Theses'. It spelled out the policy and direction the Bolshevik Party should take towards its revolutionary goals. In Lenin's 'April Theses' which was also published in Pravda, the document stated there should be no support for the Provisional Government and all power should be transferred to the Soviets. He also stated that all of the landlord's estates should be confiscated, all land should be nationalized, there should be a single national bank, and he wanted an end to the imperialist world war. In addition he stated, "I am coming to the last point, the name of our Party. We must call ourselves the Communist Party – just as Marx and Engels called themselves Communists."

On April 27, 1917, Lenin was Chairman of the Petrograd City Conference of the RSDLP (Bolsheviks) and his resolutions for the Party were adopted.

On June 16, 1917, Lenin attended the First All-Russian Congress of the Soviet of Workers' and Soldiers' Deputies in Petrograd. The Bolsheviks had only 105 delegates out of more than a thousand at the Congress. After the Menshevik leader stated that there is no Party in Russia prepared to assume full power, Lenin retorted, "Yes, there is. No party can refuse this, and our Party certainly doesn't. It is ready to take over full power at any moment."

On July 20, 1917, the government issued a warrant for the arrest of twenty-eight prominent Bolsheviks including Lenin. Lenin and the other Bolshevik leaders were held on charges of high treason as accomplices for the Germans. The Provisional Government stated that the Bolshevik leaders were German agents working on orders from the German general staff. As result of this, Lenin escaped to Razliv, twenty miles northwest of Petrograd and stayed there with fellow Bolshevik Grigory Zinoviev hiding in a hay-covered hut in the wilderness. Lenin continued to write articles while in hiding. By the end of August, Lenin left Razliv and moved to Finland. In order to fool the authorities, Lenin had a false name put on his papers and he shaved off his beard and wore a wig as a disguise.

On October 20, 1917, Lenin left Finland and returned to Petrograd. On October 23, 1917, Lenin attended a meeting of the Central Committee of the Bolshevik Party and stated that he supports an armed insurrection. Many of the members of

Lenin Studying at Razliv Statue by Zavalov, c. 1966. **$275-$295**
Aluminum, 10 1/4" x 7 1/4".
Engraving: Soviet Army Day, 1966.

the Central Committee were hesitant and resisted the proposal of an armed insurrection but after ten hours of deliberation Lenin's resolution was adopted. On November 6, 1917, Lenin wrote a 'Letter to Central Committee Members' stating, "The situation is extremely critical. It is clear as can be that delaying the uprising now really means death. … We must not wait! We may lose everything." This message was sent from the apartment of a Bolshevik comrade where he was hiding for almost two weeks. That evening Lenin put on a disguise to prevent him from being discovered and arrested. He found his way to the Smolny Institute, the Bolshevik headquarters, to join the leadership of the uprising. At 2:00 am, November 7, 1917 (October 25 old calendar), Trotsky the head of the Military Revolutionary Committee which planned the operation of the insurrection told Lenin, "It's begun." With little resistance the Bolsheviks stormed the Winter Palace the house of the Provisional Government and it was overthrown. Lenin remarked to Trotsky, "The transition from illegality and being hounded from pillar to post to power is too abrupt. It makes me dizzy."

Replica of the Statue of Lenin by V.V. Kozlov outside the Smolny Institute in Leningrad (now St. Petersburg) by Murzin, c. 1977. **$175-$225**
Aluminum, 9 1/2" x 3 1/4".
Text: 1917-1927 Long Live the Dictatorship of the Proletariat.

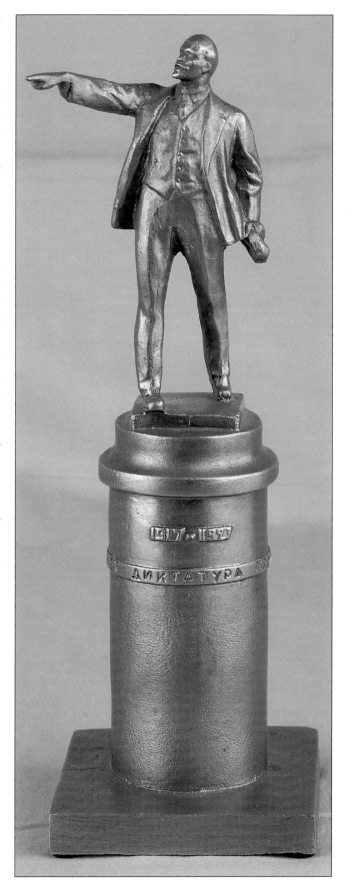

That morning at 10:00 am, Lenin made an appeal to the citizens of Russia in which he proclaimed the fall of the Provisional Government. He stated, "The immediate offer of a democratic peace, the abolition of landed proprietorship, workers' control over production and the establishment of Soviet power – this cause had been secured. Long live the revolution of workers, soldiers and peasants!"

At 10:30 pm that evening, the Second Congress of Soviets convened in the great white ballroom of the Smolny Institute. In protest to the Bolshevik seizure of power, many of the Socialist Revolutionary delegates walked out of the Congress an indication of the rift that existed between the Bolsheviks and the other left-wing parties. Nevertheless, there was a great reception when Lenin stepped onto the podium. When the ovation subsided Lenin said, "We shall now proceed to construct the socialist order." Lenin announced his plan for peace and the end of the war. The Decree on Land was also announced which would abolish land proprietorship. The land would be turned over to the Soviet of Peasants Deputies.

Also at the Second Congress, members of the Council of People's Commissars (Sovnarkom) were announced and Lenin was the Chairman of the Council. Several weeks after the Congress, seven Left Socialist Revolutionaries were given portfolios as Commissars. Of the 100 members of the government of the Republic, the Bolsheviks held seventy seats, while the remaining seats were held by other factions. Trotsky stated that the government welcomed all parties and groups which would adopt its programmes. The Council of People's Commissars (Sovnarkom) ordered a decree signed by Lenin that there would be free elections for the Constituent Assembly, which would be held on November 25, 1917. Lenin endorsed this election to promote social democracy within the country. When the coun-

Leningrad. Smolny Commemorative Pin, c. 1970s-1980s. **$5-$10**

Award Plaque Showing the Painting of Lenin in his office in the Smolny Institute by I. Brodsky c. 1954, 13" x 9". **$35-$40**

try-wide election was completed and the votes counted, the Socialist Revolutionaries held a large majority of the 707 seats in the Constituent Assembly. The Bolsheviks obtained only twenty-five percent of the seats in the house, while the Socialist Revolutionaries had almost twice that amount. The remaining seats in the Constituent Assembly were held by other parties and groups. On January 18, 1918, the Constituent Assembly convened at the Tauride Palace in Petrograd. A motion to ratify Bolshevik decrees which were announced by Lenin at the Second Congress of Soviets were defeated. The Bolsheviks and the Left Socialist Revolutionaries, a splinter group of the Socialist Revolutionaries, walked-out and the Constituent Assembly was dissolved. The Bolsheviks declared the Constituent Assembly 'counterrevolutionary'. Lenin commented, "The dispersal of the Constituent Assembly by Soviet authority means a complete and frank liquidation of the ideas of formal democracy in the name of revolutionary dictatorship. It will serve as a good lesson."

On January 24, 1918, the Bolsheviks opened the Third All-Russian Congress of Soviets. The Bolsheviks had slightly more than fifty percent of the delegates at this Congress. The Congress ratified all resolutions and laws announced by the Bolsheviks. The Congress established itself as the new permanent government of Russia.

The rift that developed between the Bolsheviks and the other socialist parties of the Constituent Assembly widened until they could not see eye-to-eye and an immense division developed. The revolution spread successfully in the large cities of central Russia which were more industrialized but there was a heavy resistance in the rural areas and distant regions of the country. The difference in ideologies eventually erupted into the two-year Civil War, commonly known as the 'Whites' against the 'Reds'. The Bolshevik Red Army, which was formed in January 1918, received its directions from the Military Revolutionary Committee which was under the direction of the Central Committee of the Communist Party. Trotsky was the Commissar of War and was the head of the Military Revolutionary Committee.

After the revolution there was a growing hostility between the capitalists and the plant managers towards the Bolshevik regime. To combat this, workers' factory committees were created to control management and create factory policy. Unfortunately, there was a lack of workers' discipline within the factories and the workers' performance was unsatisfactory to meet production requirements. By March 1918, 'bourgeois specialists' which were former factory managers and owners during the czarist regime, that were willing to cooperate with the Bolsheviks, were utilized to help run the factories to increase productivity, which was badly needed during the Civil War effort.

At the same time, the peasants in the countryside were not delivering the food required to feed the army and the workers in the cities. The peasants had no incentive to grow and deliver more produce, as the government could not provide the consumer and industrial goods in return. The government was issuing paper money in return, but it was essentially worthless.

During the Civil War the Bolsheviks had to resort to an economic policy called 'War Communism'. 'War Communism' was a period of extreme communism that lasted throughout the Civil War. Stringent economic centralization was introduced. Industrial production was allocated to the Civil War effort and compulsory requisitioning of food from the peasants to the people in the cities was decreed. These emergency measures were necessary to help the Bolsheviks during the Civil War.

Lenin desperately wanted a peace with Germany, which would give the Bolshevik Red Army the ability to concentrate on the Civil War at hand. Trotsky and other Bolshevik leaders worked feverishly on a treaty to end their war with Germany. On March 3, 1918, the Brest-Litovsk Treaty was signed. Lenin through the agreement in the treaty gave up major land concessions to achieve the peace that would protect the new Bolshevik regime. On March 14, 1918, at the Fourth Congress of Soviets Lenin stated, "In view of the fact that we have no army, that our troops at the front are in a most demoralized condition, and that we must make use of every possible breathing-spell to retard imperialist attacks on the Soviet Socialist Republic, the Congress resolves to accept the most onerous and humiliating peace treaty which the Soviet Government signed with Germany." Fortunately for Lenin the Brest-Litovsk Treaty was nullified two days after the Germans surrendered to the allies on November 11, 1918, and all the land concessions to the Germans were alleviated. This change of events had a very positive effect for Lenin politically.

On March 10, 1918, Lenin moved the capital of Russia from Petrograd to Moscow. The purpose of the move was to put the capital farther away from the border of Europe in fear

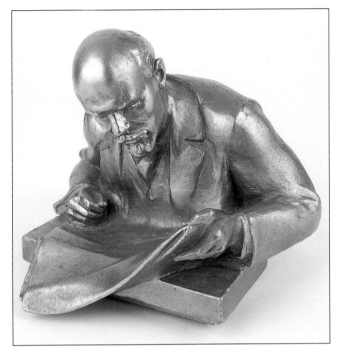

Lenin at His Desk Reading the Newspaper 'Pravda' Statue, c. 1970s-1980s. **$165-$185**
Aluminum, 6 1/2" x 7 1/2".

Photograph of Lenin Reading the Newspaper 'Pravda' at his office in the Kremlin October 1918 Moscow by P. Otsup.

One Ruble Coin Commemorating the Games of the XXII Olympiad Moscow, coin issued 1978. Coin shows the Kremlin Towers. **$10-$15**

capitalism but it would be controlled, so it would not destroy the fundamentals of socialism within the country. He stated, "Of course, freedom of trade means growth of capitalism. If there are small enterprises, if there is freedom of exchange – capitalism will appear. But is this capitalism dangerous to us, if we keep our hands on the factories, the transportation system and foreign trade? I believe that this capitalism is not dangerous to us… Is state capitalism dangerous to us? No, because we will decide in what measure we shall grant concessions." With respect to the peasants, "Let us revise our policy towards the peasants … Why do we propose to abolish requisitioning? Because we must give back to the small-holder a stimulus, an incentive, and a push."

The NEP that Lenin introduced was an example of Lenin's flexibility to make adjustments when necessary to improve the state of Russia's economy. On July 5, 1921, Lenin spoke at the Comintern (Communist International) Congress stating, "We are not alone in the world. We exist as a link of the world economy in a chain of capitalist states." On October 29, 1921, at a conference in Moscow he said, "The development of small commercial enterprises, the leasing of State enterprises, etc. means the development of capitalist relations and this is dangerous; but there is just no other way." Later on December 30, 1921, Lenin drafted a resolution on the role and function of the trade unions under the NEP. In it he stated, "The transfer of enterprises to profit and loss means that with regards to socialized enterprises, it is undoubtedly the duty of the trade unions to protect the interests of the working people, to facilitate as far as possible the improvement of their standard of living, and constantly to correct the blunders and excesses of business organizations resulting from bureaucratic distortions of the State apparatus." Lenin vigorously supported the NEP as a vehicle to improve Russia's economy and he would have no doubt continued to promote the concepts of socialism for the country and its people.

The stresses during the revolution and the ensuing Civil War caused Lenin's health to deteriorate towards the end of the 1920s. Lenin suffered from insomnia, lack of concentration and headaches, which started to affect his ability in running the country. In July 1921, Lenin's health deteriorated so much that he needed a month's holiday. At various points during the year 1922, Lenin continued to suffer from ill heath. The doctors started to suspect that a bullet embedded in his body as a result of Fanya Kaplan's assassination attempt, started to develop an abscess which may have been disturbing his nervous system. On April 23, 1922, the bullet was removed surgi-

Coat-of-Arms of the USSR, c. 1950s-1960s. **$135-$185**
Cast aluminum, 13" x 10 1/4".
Was mounted externally on government buildings, post offices, railway trains, etc.

cally. On May 26, 1922, Lenin had his first stroke due to arteriosclerosis of the brain. As a result of the stroke, he was partially paralyzed and he also suffered from a speech impediment for a short time. Against doctor's orders he continued to work as much as possible but by the end of the year his health continued to deteriorate. On December 13, 1922, Lenin suffered two attacks, which were diagnosed as thrombosis of the brain. During the night of December 15-16, 1922, he suffered from an attack that lasted over an hour. This was his second stroke, which paralyzed his right arm and leg. It made work more difficult and confined him to his bed for longer periods of time. He now had to resort to dictating his letters to his secretary as it was difficult for him to write. He was only allowed five to ten minutes dictation time per day, as doctors required him to get as much rest as possible.

On December 23, 1922, the Tenth All-Russian Congress of Soviets opened at the Bolshoi Theatre in Moscow. At the Congress a declaration was presented for the amalgamation of the Russian Socialist Federative Soviet Republic, the Ukrainian Socialist Soviet Republic, the Transcaucasian Socialist Federative Republic, and the Byelorussian Socialist Soviet Republic into the Union of Soviet Socialist Republics (USSR). Unfortunately, Lenin could not attend due to his illness.

On December 30, 1922, at the First Congress of Soviets of the USSR, the Declaration and the Union Treaty on the formation of the USSR was signed and the USSR was born. Unfortunately, Lenin was confined to his bed and could not attend.

Cast Aluminum Wall Plaques that were mounted externally on government buildings, c. 1947.
1. Order of Lenin, 4 1/4" x 4 1/4". **$65-$85**
2. Order of Red Banner Labour, 4 1/4" x 3 1/2". **$65-$85**

Coat-of-Arms of the USSR, c. 1970s-1980s.
1. Cast aluminum, 9 1/4" x 8 3/4". **$75-$95**
Was mounted externally on government buildings.
2. Solid wood, 10 3/4" x 10". **$75-$95**
Was mounted on office walls, podiums in government buildings.

USSR Pins, c. 1970s-1980s. **$5-$10**

USSR Coat-of-Arms Badge, c. 1970s-1980s. **$10-$15**

Republics of the USSR Pin Set, c. 1980s. **$35-$45**

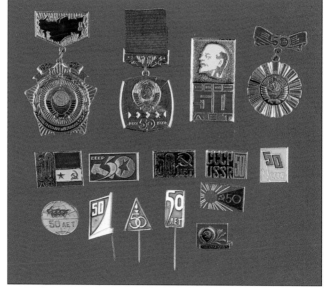

50th Year of the Formation of the USSR Pins, c. 1972. **$5-$10**

Order of the Friendship of Peoples. **$235-$295**
Awarded for the development of cooperation between socialist nations and peoples. Instituted December 17, 1972 for the 50th Year of the formation of the USSR and approximately 100,000 were issued.

60th Year of the Formation of the USSR Pins, c. 1982. **$5-$10**

60th Year of the Formation of the USSR 1922-1982 Table Medallion, c. 1982. **$85-$115**
Text on back: 60th Year of the Union of Soviet Socialist Republics.

One Ruble Coin Commemorating the 60th Year of the Formation of the USSR, coin issued 1982. **$10-$15**
Text on front: 60th Year of the Union of Soviet Socialist Republics.

Union of Inviolable Free Republics Badge, c. 1970s-1980s. **$15-$20**

USSR 1970 Census Badge, c.1970. **$15-$20**
Text: All-Union Census of the Population.

Silk Award Pennant with USSR Coat-of-Arms, c. 1970s-1980s. **$15-$20**
17 1/2" x 13".
A blank pennant could be used to attach award pins and badges.

Flags of the USSR.
1. c. 1950s, 116" x 58". **$165-$195**
2. c. 1960s, 58" x 30". **$85-$115**
3. c. 1989, 60' x 30". Manufactured by the Main Moscow District Industry (Glavmosmestprom) Factory Soviet Army. **$45-$65**
4. Car and Desk Flags. **$35-$45**

Statue of Lenin Commemorating the 1st All-Russian Agricultural Exhibition in Moscow, 1923 by Flekht c. 1923, 17 1/2" x 6". **$450-$575**
Heavy alloy and enamel coating.
Text on front: Vladimir Ilyich Lenin.
Text on back: In Remembrance of the 1st All-Russian Agricultural and Shrub Industry Exhibition USSR Moscow 1923.

As Lenin's health continued to deteriorate, Stalin's ambitions to take over leadership of the Party grew. During the Eleventh Party Congress on March 27, 1922, Stalin who was already a member of the Politburo, was elected General Secretary of the Party. He was already Commissar for the Nationalities and also Commissar for the Workers' and Peasants' Inspectorate. All of these appointments combined gave Stalin extraordinary power, which he would ultimately use to take over control of the Party.

Trotsky and Stalin were bitter enemies right from the earliest days of their careers as revolutionaries. Trotsky's rise to power grew quickly as he was the President of the St. Petersburg Soviet of Workers' Deputies in 1905 after the 'Bloody Sunday' Revolution. He was always next in power to Lenin at the Smolny Institute the Bolshevik headquarters, during the early days of the Revolution of 1917. Trotsky became Commissar of War and built the Red Army, which was victorious in the Civil War under his leadership, which assured the Bolshevik's establishing the new government. Meanwhile, Stalin rose within the ranks of the Party slowly in a more cunning way, with a strategy of eventually taking over power of the Party.

Towards the later months of 1922, the issue of the State's foreign trade monopoly surfaced. Lenin was confined to his quarters due to his illness and had to dictate letters to Trotsky, which would then be forwarded to the Central Committee to persuade their vote on this issue. Lenin wanted the State's foreign trade monopoly to continue as it was a great source of revenue for the State. On December 21, 1922, Lenin dictated a note to his wife Krupskaya for Trotsky, thanking him for his support and victory in the vote of the Central Committee on this issue. Lenin at this time was under doctor's orders to rest and refrain from his work as much as possible. Stalin was consolidating his power within the Party and did not want Trotsky to be involved with Lenin and furthermore, wanted Lenin as far removed from politics as possible. Stalin lashed out at Krupskaya on the phone with verbal abuse and threats for taking down Lenin's letter written for Trotsky, which was in defiance of the doctor's orders for him to rest. Lenin was not prepared to accept such treatment to himself or his wife and this was one of the contributing factors that caused Lenin to write his 'Testament'. Lenin became alarmed by the way in which Stalin had patiently built-up both the power and authority of his office and his own personal standing within the Party. Stalin now became a leading figure within the Party. Even with Lenin being so ill, he could sense that he did not like these developments and became mistrustful of Stalin's personality. Another concern for Lenin was the 'split' developing within the Central Committee and the Party as a consequence of the hatred between Stalin and Trotsky.

Lenin started to deplore Stalin after the Krupskaya telephone incident and on December 23, 1922, he immediately started dictating his 'Letter to the Congress' known as the 'Testament' to his secretary. On January 4, 1923, Lenin wrote a postscript which condemned Stalin even further. Lenin made it clear to his secretary that the 'Testament' was to be "kept in a special place under special responsibility" and to be considered categorically secret. He asked that the sealed envelope which had the copies of the document within it, should be marked to the effect that it could only be opened by Lenin, and after his death by his secretary. In the December 'Testament' Lenin wrote of Stalin, "Comrade Stalin, having become Secretary-General, has unlimited authority concentrated in his hands, and I am not sure whether he will always be capable of using that authority with sufficient caution." Even with Lenin's ill-health he appeared to be aware of the future direction the Party would take under Stalin's control. In the postscript of January 4, 1923, he condemned Stalin further by writing, "Stalin is too rude and this defect, although quite tolerable in our midst and in dealings among Communists, becomes intolerable in a Secretary-General. That is why I suggest that the comrades think about a way of removing Stalin from that post and appointing another man in his stead who in all other respects differs from Comrade Stalin in having only one advantage, namely, that of being more tolerant, more loyal, more polite and considerate to the comrades, less capricious, etc."

On March 9, 1923, Lenin had his third stroke, which confined him to his bed. Lenin's right arm and leg were paralyzed, he lost his ability to speak, and he was starting to lose consciousness. On May 15, 1923, Lenin was moved from Moscow to his state home in Gorki to rest. On October 19, 1923, Lenin was driven back to Moscow by car. He went to his flat and his office in the Kremlin for the last time. On his way back to Gorki, Lenin insisted that his chauffeur drive him through the First All-Russian Agricultural Exhibition so he could see the festivities. Some of the spectators at the exhibition recognized him in the back seat of the car and started to wave and cheer at him as he drove by. Because of his illness he was unable to step out of the car and meet the people.

On January 21, 1924, Vladimir Lenin had another attack and died at 5:50 pm. Before the body was moved to Moscow an autopsy was performed. Lenin died from severe sclerosis of

1924 Coins USSR (Union of Soviet Socialist Republics).
These were the first silver ruble coins issued in the USSR and show the first variation of its Coat-of-Arms with six ribbons representing the first republics of the union.
1. One-half of a Ruble, 50 Kopeck. **$20-$30**
2. One Ruble. **$55-$75**
Text on front: Workers of All Countries, Unite!

Left: Lenin Mausoleum Pin, c. 1970s-1980s. **$5-$10**
Right: 10th Anniversary of Lenin's Death Commemorative Badge, c. 1934.
$125-$145

Copper Lenin Wall Plaque c. 1940s-1950s, 32" x 27". Was mounted externally on the wall of a Soviet government building. **$1850-$2500**

Copper Lenin Wall Plaque c. 1970s, 20" diameter. Was mounted internally on the wall of a Soviet government boardroom of the Central Committee of the CPSU. **$250-$325**

the arteries leading to the brain. The arteries had calcified and prevented normal flow of blood and the necessary amount of oxygen from reaching the brain. On January 23, 1924, Lenin's body was brought from Gorki to Moscow where it was to lie in state. Thereafter, was the embalming of Lenin's body and its removal to a new mausoleum in Red Square.

Prior to his death, Lenin stated that he wanted to be buried next to his mother in St. Petersburg. On January 30, 1924, Lenin's wife Krupskaya wrote an article in Pravda pleading that Lenin's body should not be embalmed in a mausoleum stating, "I have a great request to make of you: do not allow your grief for Ilyich to express itself in the external veneration of his person." Regardless of Lenin's request and Krupskaya's statements, on March 25, 1924, the Commission for the Immortalization of the Memory of V.I. Ulyanov (Lenin) began planning a new mausoleum, which finally opened on August 1, 1924.

After Lenin's death the struggle for the leadership of the Party began between the two rivals Trotsky and Stalin. The bitter disagreements Lenin had with Stalin remained unknown to the general population and was only known to leading members of the Party. Stalin outmaneuvered Trotsky by joining forces with Kamenev and Zinoviev forming a 'troika' of power. Kamenev and Zinoviev joined Stalin in believing it would help their future positions within the Party, as Stalin was already the General-Secretary. The three collectively having the most power in the Party decided that Lenin's 'Testament' should not be read at the Thirteenth Party Congress. The 'Testament' was read at a plenary session of the Central Committee in May 1924. The Central Committee finally decided at the meeting that the 'Testament' should not be read at the Congress and should only be communicated confidentially to selected delegates. This was a great victory for Stalin and from that point onwards he began to consolidate his power within the Party.

Unfortunately, during the last year of Lenin's life he was unable to effectively run the country due the severity of his illness. During the reforms of the NEP, the economy and life for the Soviet citizens improved dramatically. We will never know the further direction Lenin would have taken as the leader of the USSR, or for that matter, if Trotsky would have become Lenin's successor.

Through Stalin's dictatorship, not through the Communist Party itself, he completely distorted the virtuous ideals of socialism that were envisioned by the revolutionaries, by enveloping Soviet society with terror and abhorrent crimes to humanity unparalleled in history. What transpired when Stalin

Bronze Bas-Relief of Lenin with Award Box, c. 1949. **$85-$95**

eventually took power in 1929, was the forced collectivization of the farms and the creation of a forced industrialized economy. The treaty of Brest-Litovsk and the NEP are examples of Lenin's flexibility when dealing with economic and political issues. There is no doubt that Lenin still would have promoted socialism as the better way for the nation and its people but it would have undoubtedly been achieved in a more civilized way.

"BARELEF" Bas-Relief of Lenin Table or Wall Plaques by N. Sokolov, c. 1980s. Manufactured at the Leningrad Mint, 4" diameter. **$35-$45**

Lenin Table Medallion in Plastic Case, c. 1970s. **$35-$45**

Lenin with Cap Table Medallion, c. 1970s. **$55-$65**
Aluminum, 4" diameter.
Text on back: We Speak – Lenin,
We Mean – Party,
We Speak – Party,
We Mean – Lenin.

Order of Lenin. **$550-$750**
Highest award of the USSR. Awarded for outstanding achievements in the
revolutionary movement, labour activity, defence of the socialist homeland
and other contributions for the Soviet government and society. The Order of
Lenin is presented to individuals entitled 'Hero of the Soviet Union' or 'Hero
of Socialist Labour'. Instituted April 6, 1930 and over 460,000 were issued.
1. Large oval version on ribbon suspension, c. 1950s-1991.

Order of Lenin Pin, c. 1970s. **$15-$20**

Bas-Relief of Lenin Wall Plaque, c. 1930s. **$95-$115**
Cast aluminum, 9 3/4" x 8".

Statue of Lenin on marble base, c. 1930s. **$285-$315**
Heavy nickel alloy, 14 1/2" x 5 1/2".

Sold Aluminum Bust of Lenin, c. 1930s. **$245-$265**
7 1/2" x 5 1/2".

Porcelain Bust of Lenin by Mamok, c. 1933. **$250-$325**
10" x 7".

Statue of Lenin on stone base by Vik Korol, c. 1936. **$175-$215**
Bronze, 9 1/4" x 2 1/2".

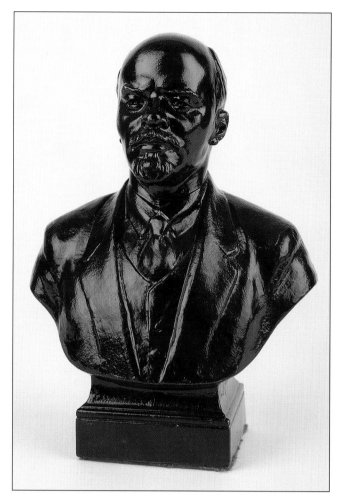

Bust of Lenin by L. Paidonin, c. 1940s. **$195-$245**
Painted nickel alloy, 9" x 6 1/2".

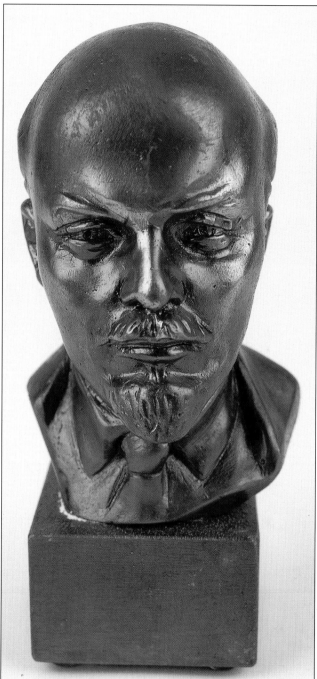

Bronze Bust of Lenin, Moscow c. 1955. **$135-$155**
5 1/2" x 2 1/2".

Bust of Lenin c. 1950s, 7 1/4" x 5 3/4".
1. Porcelain. **$145-$170**
2. Aluminum. **$135-$165**

Bust of Lenin by Gerasimenko, c. 1950s-1960s. **$115-$145**
Bronze, 3 3/4" x 2 3/4".

Bust of Lenin by Starostin, c. 1950s. **$165-$185**
Aluminum, 7 1/2" x 4 3/4".

Busts of Lenin, c. 1950s-1960s. **$115-$145**
Nickel alloy, 5 1/4" x 3 1/4".

Bust of Lenin, c. 1968. **$75-$85**
Solid plaster, 6 1/2" x 4 1/4".

Bust of Lenin, c. 1960s. **$125-$165**
Solid white plastic mold, 12" x 4 1/2".

Bronze Bust of Lenin by Petrov, c. 1960s-1970s. **$185-$215**
7 1/2" x 5 1/4".

Plaster Bust of Lenin by V. Aksyanov, c. 1970. **$265-$295**
13" x 10 1/4".
Artistic Fund RSFSR Moscow Division Sculpture Manufacturing Factory.

Bust of Lenin c. 1967, 5 1/4" x 4".
1. Solid white plastic mold. **$65-$85**
2. Heavy zinc alloy. This bust was dedicated on 20/11/1969. **$135-$185**

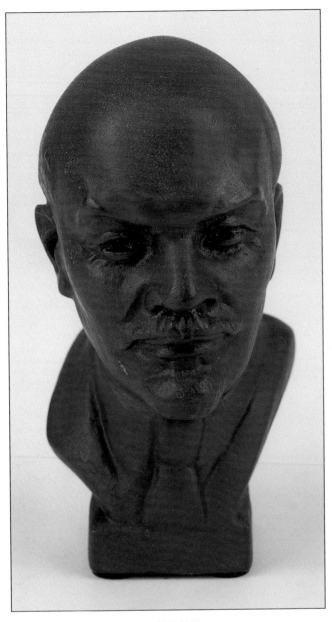

Busts of Lenin by Z. Lerner, c. 1970s.
Bronze.
1. 3 1/2" x 2". **$75-$95**
2. 4" x 2 3/4". **$85-$115**

Bust of Lenin by Tvneta, c. 1970s. **$115-$135**
Bronze, 4" x 2".

Bust of Lenin on stone base by Lubrovich, c. 1970s. **$125-$145**
Bronze, 4 1/4" x 2 1/4".

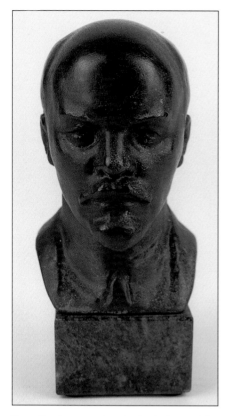

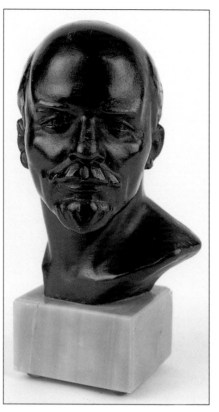

Bust of Lenin on stone base by Geodzhian, c. 1970s. **$125-$145**
Nickel alloy, 4 3/4" x 2 1/4".

Bust of Lenin on stone base by Artamonov, c. 1970s. **$125-$145**
Nickel alloy, 6" x 3".

Bust of Lenin by Gevorkian, c. 1970s-1980s. **$95-$115**
Nickel alloy, 5 1/2" x 3 1/4".

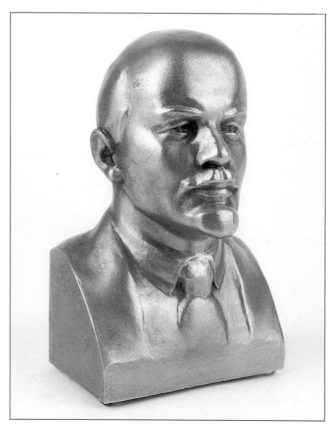

Bust of Lenin, c. 1972. **$135-$155**
Aluminum, 6 3/4" x 4 1/4".
This bust was dedicated in the 50th Year of the USSR.

Sculptures by Zavalov.
1. Statue of Lenin with Note Pad, c. 1960s-1970s. Nickel alloy, 14 1/4" x 5".
$195-$235
2. Bust of Lenin, ca 1960s-1970s. Nickel alloy, 9" x 5 1/2". **$185-$235**
3. Bust of Lenin, c. 1985. Aluminum, 8 3/4" x 6". **$175-$215**

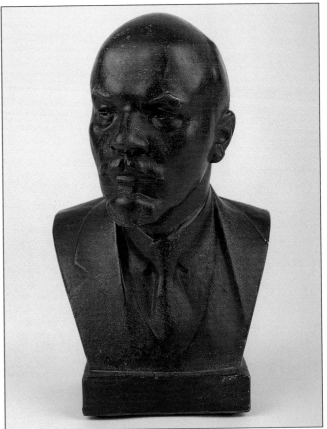

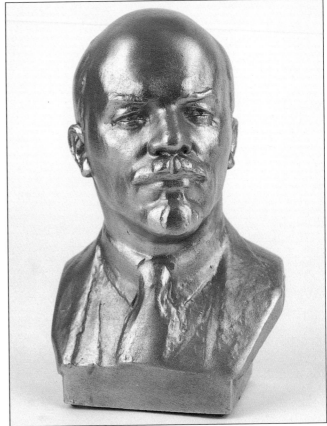

Busts of Lenin by V. Sichev.
Aluminum.
1. c. 1961, 10" x 5". "Monumentsculptura" Leningrad. **$245-$265**
2. c. 1970s-1980s, 10 1/4" x 6 1/2". **$265-$295**
3. c. 1970s-1980s, 10" x 6 1/2". **$225-$245**
4. c. 1975, 8 1/4" x 4 1/4". **$145-$165**

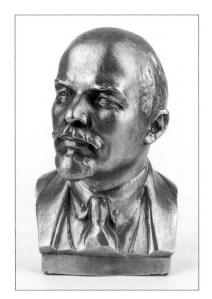

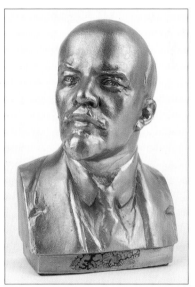

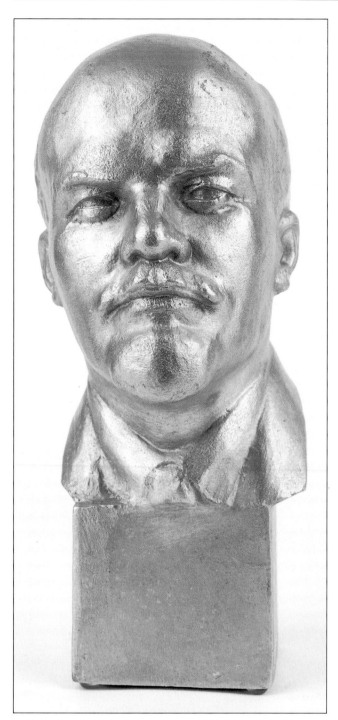

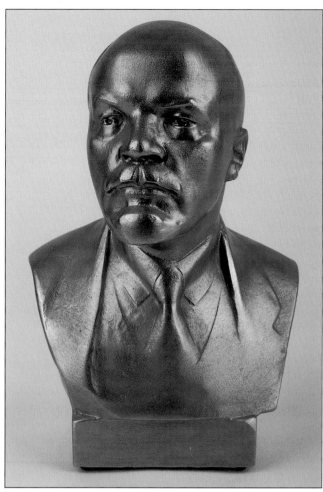

Bust of Lenin by N. Baganov, c. 1975. **$175-$215**
Aluminum, 8 3/4" x 5 1/2".

Bust of Lenin, c. 1970s-1980s. **$230-$265**
Aluminum, 10 1/2" x 4 1/4".

Bust of Lenin, c. 1970s-1980s. **$175-$215**
Aluminum, 9" x 6".

Busts of Lenin by AO (initials).
Aluminum.
1. c. 1976, 9 1/2" x 5". **$185-$235**
2. On marble base c. 1970s, 10" x 4 1/4". **$185-$230**

Bust of Lenin by SL (initials), c. 1976. **$115-$135**
Aluminum, 6 1/4" x 4 1/4".

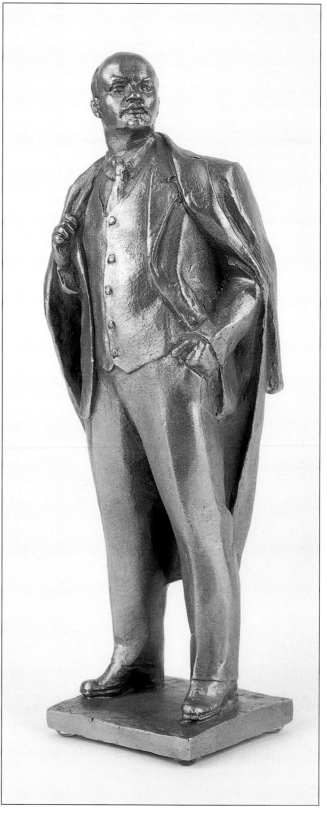

Sculptures by A. Murzin.
Aluminum.
1. Bust of Lenin c. 1977, 8 1/4" x 8 1/2". **$220-$265**
2. Statue of Lenin with Overcoat c. 1987, 10" x 3 1/2". **$220-$245**

Bust of Lenin with Cap, c. 1970s-1980s. **$155-$175**
Aluminum, 6 1/2" x 3".

Bust of Lenin by V. Yudin, c. 1977. **$175-$195**
Plaster, 9 1/2" x 5 1/2".
Artistic Fund RSFSR Moscow Division
Sculpture Manufacturing Division.

Photograph of Lenin with cap May, 1919 by A. Savelyev.

Busts of Lenin by Volkov, c. 1980. **$165-$195**
Nickel alloy, 8 3/4" x 6 1/2".

Lenin and Banner Statue by B. V. Yedunov, c. 1970s-1980s. **$295-$360**
Aluminum, 15" x 10".

Lenin Sitting and Reading Statue, c. 1970s-1980s. **$245-$285**
Aluminum, 11" x 6".

Lenin Sitting with Overcoat in a Revolutionary Pose Statue, c. 1970s-1980s.
$165-$185
Aluminum, 8" x 8 1/2".

Below:
Statues of Lenin, c. 1970s-1980s.
Aluminum.
1. 13" x 5 1/2". **$185-$215**
2. 6" x 2". **$55-$65**

Lenin with Note Pad Statue, c. 1976. **$220-$235**
Aluminum, 12 1/2" x 4 1/2".

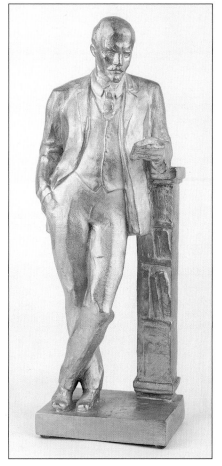

Pages 60-62: An Assortment of Lenin Pins from the 1950s to the 1980s. Lenin pins were worn by Soviet citizens to show their allegiance to the Party. **$5-$10**

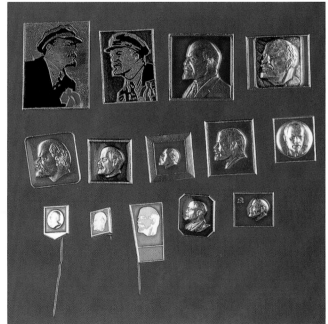

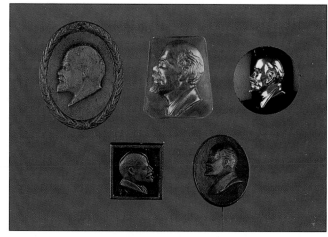

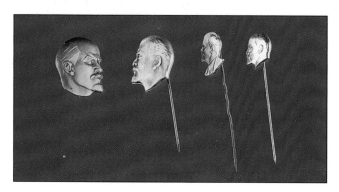

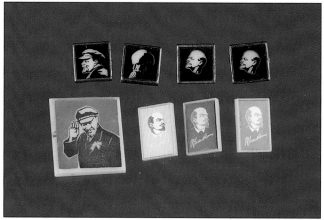

THREE

THE POLITICAL SYSTEM OF THE USSR

There were two major bodies that formed the political system of the USSR. The supreme body was the Communist Party of the Soviet Union (CPSU) and working along side with it and subordinate to it was the Soviet Government. The CPSU proposed policy and the Soviet Government implemented it. The officials who ran the CPSU also controlled the Soviet Government. As a result of changes in policies and leadership, the Soviet political system had changes made to it throughout the decades. The following is the format of the Soviet political system at the time of the Brezhnev era.

The Communist Party of the Soviet Union (CPSU)

As stated in the Constitution of the USSR adopted by the Supreme Soviet on October, 1977: The leading and guiding force of the Soviet society and the nucleus of its political system, of all state organizations and public organizations, is the CPSU. The CPSU exists for the people and serves the people. The Communist Party, armed with Marxism-Leninism, directs the great constructive work of the Soviet people in the struggle for the victory of communism.

Almost ten percent of the adult population were members of the CPSU and they were recruited from all segments of society. Being a member of the Party usually ensured career advancement and was necessary for citizens with political ambitions. All members belonged to one of the approximately 400,000 primary Party organizations based at workplaces throughout the country. From there the Party hierarchy was in the shape of a pyramid, moving through city, district, regional and republic levels to the Central Committee, which was made

up of approximately 500 members elected every five years to represent all of the areas of the USSR.

We will examine the pyramid structure of the CPSU starting at its apex and work our way down. At the apex of the pyramid is the head of the Party, the General Secretary. This was the most powerful position in the USSR. The CPSU and the Soviet Government were intertwined, as it was quite common for the General Secretary to hold the highest positions in the Soviet Government as well. Examples of General Secretaries of the past were Vladimir Lenin, Joseph Stalin, Nikita Khrushchev, Leonid Brezhnev, and Mikhail Gorbachev, who was the last General Secretary of the USSR.

The General Secretary was chairman of the Politburo, which met weekly and was the major policy making body of the Party and in effect the country. The Politburo had between

Communist Party of the Soviet Union (CPSU) Pins, c. 1970s-1980s. **$5-$10**

eleven and sixteen members and approximately a third of them held key posts in the Soviet Government as well. Members of the Politburo were selected by the General Secretary on the basis of their loyalty, political and administrative abilities. The Politburo was a highly secretive organization. An example of this was the unexpected removal of Nikita Khrushchev in October 1964 and his being replaced by Leonid Brezhnev as General Secretary. In October 1952, Stalin changed the name of the Politburo to the Presidium. In April 1966, Brezhnev reinstated the name Politburo again.

The General Secretary also presided over the next important policy-making body of the Party, the Secretariat of the Central Committee of the CPSU. The Secretariat was the administrative head of the CPSU and provided daily direction and leadership of the Party. The Secretariat checked on and ensured the implementation of policy by Party, governmental, and other institutions. It was also responsible for the trade unions, courts, police, the armed forces, health and social welfare, and propaganda.

The next important policy-making body after the Secretariat was the Central Committee of the CPSU. The Central Committee was made up of approximately 500 members representing all regions of the USSR, selected every five years at the Party Congress. The Central Committee directed the entire work of the Party in the intervals between Party Congresses. It directed the work of all central governmental and public organizations through the Party organizations that were within them. The members of the Central Committee represent the most influential element of the Party, the government, trade unions, armed forces, and other organizations. According to the Party statute, the Central Committee was to convene in a plenary session twice a year.

The last and largest member of the CPSU was the Party Congress, which could have up to 5,000 members. The Party Congress convened once every five years, though it varied.

Communist Party Political Banner, c. 1970s-1980s. **$115-$155**
Silk, 69" x 40".
Slogans on front -
Top left: Workers of All Countries, Unite!
Bottom: Turn Plans of the Party into Reality!
Text on back: Glory Union of Soviet Socialist Republics!

Since the late 1920s during the Stalin era, the Party Congress degenerated into a 'rubber stamp' organ which automatically and unanimously approved the principles and policies of the self-perpetuating Party leadership. Members of the Party Con-

Below:
Communist Party Political Banner, c. 1970s-1980s. **$115-$155**
Silk, 69" x 40".
Slogan on front: Turn Plans of the Party into Reality!
Slogan on back: Workers of All Countries, Unite!

gress were carefully selected by the Party leadership of the CPSU. The Party Congress was made up of delegates from all corners of the USSR and from all walks of Party life. The delegates provided an important means of making contact with representatives of all the regions of the USSR. They made known the policies of the CPSU, which were decided in Moscow during the Party Congress.

The National Government of the Soviet Union

The role of the National Government of the Soviet Union was to implement the policies proposed by the CPSU. The CPSU and the government were intertwined. While the Party had one head, the government had two, the Premier and the President. It was common for the General Secretary of the CPSU to hold one of these positions as well.

The Premier was the country's chief executive officer, overseeing the Presidium of the Supreme Soviet. The Presidium was a cabinet like body which had thirty-nine top Party members. The Presidium had immense powers as it issued decrees and interpreted the laws of the USSR. It had the power to appoint and dismiss military commanders. It also received foreign dignitaries and could dismiss foreign office personnel. It had the power to conclude and to break off international agreements, order mobilization of the armed forces and declare a state of war. The Presidium was a powerful body that put forth the decisions of the Party to the government. It was the Presidium of the Supreme Soviet that instituted decorations (orders and medals) and titles of honour of the USSR.

Next in the line of power in the government was the Council of Ministers which consisted of approximately 100 members, including chiefs of ministries, agencies, and commissions, along with the Premiers of the fifteen Republics of the Soviet Union. The Council of Ministers was the highest executive and administrative organ of State power in the USSR. It dealt with matters of economic, social and cultural development and defence for the State. The Council of Ministers was accountable to the Presidium of the Supreme Soviet and was appointed by the Supreme Soviet on the recommendation of the 'steering committee', the Presidium. The Council of Ministers executed the national economic plan and the State budget. The State Planning Committee (GOSPLAN) was the economic staff of the Council of Ministers. The Council of Ministers was previously called the Council of Peoples Commisars (Sovnarkom) and its name was changed in 1946.

Supreme Soviet of the USSR Delegate Badge, c. 1970s-1980s. **$115-$195**

The largest body within the government was the Supreme Soviet, which had approximately 1500 members and its Chairman was the President. The Supreme Soviet consisted of two chambers of equal rights, the Council of the Union and the Council of Nationalities. The Council of the Union had 750 members and was elected on the basis of population, one deputy per 300,000 people. The Council of Nationalities also had 750 members and was elected on a territorial basis with representatives from the Union Republics and Autonomous Republics, Regions and Districts. The term of the Supreme Soviet of the USSR was five years. Branches and organizations of the Communist Party of the Soviet Union, Komsomol (VLKSM), trade unions, collectives and military units had the right to nominate candidates for the Supreme Soviet. A delegate chosen for a position in the Supreme Soviet was selected by the district's Party Secretary. The electorate having no other choice on election day, traditionally voted over 99 per cent in favour for the single Party selected candidate in each electoral district. About a third of the 'elected' delegates to the Supreme Soviet were important Party functionaries, government ministers, top military officials, and police officers, etc. The Supreme Soviet held three or four day sessions twice a year to approve legislation

Left: Honoured Member of the Procurators (Public Prosecutors) Award Badge, c. 1970s. **$100-$125**

Right: 50th Year of the Soviet Procurators (Public Prosecutors) Award Badge, c. 1972. **$65-$85**

and the national budget. The Supreme Soviet had its own Presidium which operated as its 'steering committee' between sessions. Before its adjournment the Supreme Soviet automatically and unanimously approved the decrees of the Presidium of the Supreme Soviet, as well as the work of the Council of Ministers.

The legal system of the USSR was part of the National Government. The Supreme Court and the Soviet judicial system was an organ of State power under the guidance and control of the Communist Party of the Soviet Union (CPSU). The Supreme Court was to maintain the Soviet laws for the cause of socialism in the USSR. The Procurator-General was the chief legal officer of the Soviet government. The Procurator's office in the Union republics appointed district and local Procurators which maintained law and order of the citizens and administrators of the USSR. The Supreme Court and the Procurator-General had a term of office of five years and were elected by the Supreme Soviet.

Congresses of the Communist Party of the Soviet Union (CPSU)

The legacy of Communist Party Congresses initially started with the First Congress of the Russian Socialist Democratic Labour Party (RSDLP), which convened in March 1898 in Minsk. Only nine people attended and most of them were arrested shortly afterwards. At that time Lenin was in exile in Siberia. As a result of this small gathering of revolutionaries the Party was born.

The Second Congress of the RSDLP was held in July and August 1903, initially in Brussels and then in London. It was during this Congress that the Bolshevik-Menshevik split occurred, which had an enormous impact on the future of the Party and the revolution. The Bolsheviks led by Lenin wanted a centralized Party, which would be controlled by its leadership of dedicated professional revolutionaries which would organize the working class towards revolution. The Mensheviks led by Martov wanted a more moderate approach for the Party, allowing all the citizens that were members having a voice within the Party. Lenin believed the 'dictatorship of the proletariat' would have to be assumed by the Party as the proletariat with its lack of sophistication would be incapable of exercising the task. Their ideological differences would become irreconcilable.

At the Third Congress of the RSDLP held in April and May 1905 in London, only the Bolsheviks were present and

2nd Congress of the Russian Socialist Democratic Labour Party (RSDLP) 1903 Commemorative Pins, c. 1970s. **$5-$10**

Lenin was elected Chairman of the Congress. Lenin defended his position of 'revolutionary dictatorship' which was contrary to the Menshevik position. Lenin was elected editor of the new Bolshevik newspaper 'The Proletarian' and he became the leader of the Bolshevik Party.

The Fourth Congress of the RSDLP held in April and May 1906 in Stockholm was called the 'Unity' Congress as there was a reconciliation attempt between the Mensheviks and the Bolsheviks. Most of the resolutions adopted during the Congress reflected Menshevik views as the Mensheviks had the majority of the seats at the Congress. A combination of seven Mensheviks and three Bolsheviks formed the new joint Central Committee. Lenin was not elected to sit as a member of the Central Committee of the Party. The apparent unity at the Congress was only formal as the split between the Bolsheviks and the Mensheviks continued.

At the Fifth Congress of the RSDLP held in May and June 1907 in London, Lenin was elected to the Presidium of the Congress but this was contested by the Mensheviks. Lenin spoke on the attitude towards 'bourgeois parties' and stated that Trotsky "has come closer to our views" and "we have solidarity on fundamental points in the question of the attitude towards 'bourgeois parties'." The struggle between the Mensheviks and the Bolsheviks continued.

The Sixth Congress of the RSDLP (Bolshevik) of August 1917 was held in Petrograd. The Party had approximately 140,000 members. Lenin was absent from the Congress as he went into hiding at Razliv to avoid the Russian authorities which had issued a warrant for his arrest. Also absent from the Congress was Zinoviev who was hiding with Lenin, while Trotsky and Kamenev were both in prison. Stalin spoke at the Congress in Lenin's defence. He spoke against the Menshevik's accusations that Lenin was a German spy.

The Seventh Congress was the first Party Congress after the revolution. The Party's name was changed to the All-Russian Communist Party (Bolshevik) RCP(B) and was held in March 1918 in Petrograd. Lenin's proposal for a peace settlement with Germany was discussed to end Russia's involvement in World War I which was devastating for the country. Lenin stated that until the country had an army that was capable of fighting successfully the peace treaty was the obvious solution.

The Eighth Congress of the RCP(B) of March 1919 was held in Moscow for the first time. Lenin made Moscow the capital of Russia and moved his office to the Kremlin. Proposals at the Congress dealt with the new Party programme and the Civil War. Lenin stated that the new Party programme should be based on the fact that the "era of the world proletarian, communist revolution has begun." The 'military opposition' who were Bolsheviks, spoke against the 'military specialists' who were formerly czarist officers that were recruited to help the Bolshevik Red Army during the Civil War. Lenin and Trotsky both supported the use of the ex-czarist officers in helping in the Civil War effort. It was during this Congress that two important sub-committees of the Central Committee were instituted. The first was the Politburo, which was to deal with urgent matters of high policy and the Orgburo (Organization Bureau), which would be in charge of Party personnel. All of the following Congresses were held in Moscow from now on.

At the Ninth Congress of the RCP(B) of April 1920, some members of the Bolshevik Party opposed the 'bureaucratic centralism' that had developed within the Party. Lenin stated, "The will of a class may sometimes be carried out by a dictator, who sometimes does more alone and is frequently more necessary." It was at this Congress that the role of the trade unions surfaced. Trotsky Commissar of War, stated that it would require military methods and strict Party control of the trade unions to repair the economy after the Civil War. The trade unions wanted to control the economy but Lenin stated that the trade unions should be "schools of communism" and that the Party must have control of the economy.

The Tenth Congress of the RCP(B) of March 1921, dealt with the creation the New Economic Policy (NEP) which was endorsed by Lenin to revive the economy after 'War Communism'. The NEP, which used capitalism in a limited way to revive the economy, became a test of loyalty of the membership to the Party. Lenin stated that what is needed is "unity, discipline and restraint." Party discipline was discussed at the Congress and a resolution on Party unity was passed. It banned the creation of factions within the Party and could ultimately lead to the expulsion from it. Lenin spoke on the proposal of the substitution of a tax in kind for compulsory deliveries as an incentive for the peasants. Lenin stated, "We must adopt our State economy to the economy of the middle peasant."

At the Eleventh Congress of the RCP(B) of March and April 1922, the role of the trade unions in the NEP was tackled. An unfortunate turn in events occurred as a consequence of the NEP, the workers started to go on strike as the situation for the working class worsened. The factories were being run by 'bourgeois specialists' working for the government. The 'bourgeois specialists' were former factory managers and owners during the czarist regime. The Workers' Opposition, a group within the Party, wanted the trade unions to defend the interests of the workers and to run the factories and manage the economy. They also wanted the trade union leaders to be elected by the union membership rather than being chosen by the Party's Central Committee. This of course would be an infringement on the Party's monopoly of power. After the Congress Stalin became General Secretary of the Central Committee of the Party, a newly created position, which he would use to his benefit to eventually take over control of the Party.

At the Twelfth Congress of the RCP(B) of April 1923, the Nationality problem surfaced as Stalin wanted the Soviet Republics to be encompassed as part of the RSFSR while retaining their autonomy within it. Trotsky was receiving notes from Lenin, stating he endorsed federalism, which unified the RSFSR and the other republics into a single Union of Soviet Socialist Republics. Lenin's 'federalist' approach won over Stalin's 'autonomization'. This division enhanced the struggle between Trotsky and Stalin. Lenin was unable to attend the Congress due to his illness and Trotsky was to speak on Lenin's behalf. Trotsky though, remained silent throughout the Congress with respect to speaking about the Nationality issue. And most importantly, he refrained from mentioning Lenin's Testament, which contained Lenin's concerns about Stalin's position as General Secretary of the Party. Trotsky let this unique opportunity to attack Stalin, with the full authority of Lenin slip away. Trotsky's silence at this Congress was a great victory for Stalin.

The Thirteenth Congress of the RCP(B) of May 1924, was the first after Lenin's death and the struggle between Trotsky and Stalin continued. Trotsky criticized the Party for a political system that appointed all the secretaries of local Party organizations from above, rather than having them elected by the members of the organization. Stalin twisted Trotsky's argument by stating it violated the system that Lenin created and

Lenin/Stalin Political Banner, c. 1950s. **$495-$585**
Satin, 53" x 43".
Slogan on front: Under the Banner of Lenin-Stalin, Under the Leadership of the Communist Party – Forward, To the Victory of Communism!
Slogan on back: Workers of All Countries, Unite!
Note: 16 Republic Coat-of-Arms 1948-1956.

his precepts for the Party. During this Congress, Kamenev who chaired the Congress and Zinoviev who was speaker for the Central Committee, joined forces with Stalin who organized the Congress to form a 'troika' of power, which would ultimately lead to Trotsky's defeat.

At the Fourteenth Congress of the RCP(B) of December 1925, Stalin continued to consolidate his power within the Party. There was still the possibility that Lenin's Testament might surface and reveal Lenin's thoughts about Stalin. One of Stalin's supporters at the Congress suppressed the idea by cunningly stating that Lenin's appraisal of Stalin and the other four leaders mentioned in the Testament was undoubtedly correct, but what advantage could there be in discrediting our leaders before the masses? Attempting to put the issue to rest Stalin said, "Yes, comrades, I am a man who goes to the point and is coarse, that is true. I don't deny it." From that point on any references to the Testament stopped which was another significant victory for Stalin. To further his supremacy within the Party, he removed Kamenev and Zinoviev from their positions in the Moscow and Leningrad Party organizations respectively. To even further his power base within the Party, Stalin in 1926 had Trotsky, Kamenev and Zinoviev removed from the Politburo.

The Fifteenth Congress of the RCP(B) was held two years later in December 1927. During the previous year 1926, a 'united opposition' led by Trotsky, Kamenev, Zinoviev and Krupskaya (Lenin's wife) was formed to oppose Stalin's rule over the Party. By the 15'th Congress, 121 members of the 'united opposition' were expelled from the Party and many were arrested. Stalin was victorious and ultimately gained control of the Party. His struggle with Trotsky was now complete. It was at this Congress that the development of the first Five-Year Plan of economic development for the country was undertaken. For the USSR to become a modern industrialized nation, the primitive and inefficient individual peasant farms would have to be transformed into modernized collective farms to support the industrialized cities. The peasants would work on the collective farms, while the workers would work in the factories fulfilling the directives handed down by the State through the Five-Year Plan.

At the Sixteenth Congress of the RCP(B) of June and July 1930, Stalin became concerned about the 'right opposition' who voted against his platforms. During the Congress a resolution was passed calling for the elimination of any member of the 'right opposition' from the Party and hence they were purged. The 'purge' also included non-Party officials working in Soviet institutions.

The Seventeenth Congress of the RCP(B) of January and February 1934, was Stalin's 'Congress of Victors' which celebrated the successes of the first Five-Year Plan. Stalin received excessive praise and adulation during the Congress by the delegates. Instead of declaring a resolution usually based on the report of the Central Committee, the Congress declared "that all the Party organizations be guided in their work by the proposals and tasks presented by Comrade Stalin in his speech." Rapid industrialization and collectivization of the farms was achieved. In Stalin's speech at the Congress he stated, "During

Communist Party Political Banner, c. 1950s. **$250-$350**
Velvet, 66" x 50".
Slogans on front -
Top: Workers of All Countries, Unite!
Bottom: Under the Banner of Marxism-Leninism,
Under the Leadership of the Communist Party – Forward, To the Victory of Communism!

this period, the USSR has become radically transformed and has cast off the aspect of backwardness and medievalism. From an agrarian country, it has become an industrial country. From a country of small individual agriculture it has become a country of collective, large-scale mechanized agriculture."

There was a lapse of five years between the Seventeenth and Eighteenth Congresses as Stalin's 'purges' became the major pre-occupation during this time. The Eighteenth Congress of the RCP(B) was held in March 1939 and was the first after the height of the 'purges'. Stalin stated that "purging Soviet organizations of spies, murderers and saboteurs would lead to the strengthening of the Soviet State." During the Congress attempts were made to reassure the delegates that there would be no more 'purges' and that the errors of the past would be rectified. This reassuring message was to be conveyed to their constituents on the farms, in the factories and to military units. During the Congress the preparations for the possibility of war was also discussed.

At the Nineteenth Congress of October 1952, the Congress's name was changed from the All-Union Communist Party (Bolshevik) RCP(B) to the Communist Party of the Soviet Union (CPSU). This was done to reflect the role the Party had throughout the nation as a whole. The Nineteenth Congress convened thirteen years after the preceding Congress, which appears to be a good indication of Stalin's dictatorship over the country. Due to the pressure from members of the Politburo, Stalin reluctantly agreed to the convocation of the Congress, as his health was deteriorating and he did not have the desire to be seen publicly. It was seven years after the war and the Politburo insisted that the nation needed a new set of directives and an affirmation that the Communist Party was still the leading force of power and direction in the country.

Stalin started sensing a power struggle among the Party leadership for his throne. In conjunction to his deteriorating health, he was developing a sense of paranoia and wanted to reorganize the Party. The Congress established a new enlarged body called the Presidium of the Central Committee, which took the place of the Politburo and the Orgburo. Stalin's intention was to remove the old leadership through Party restructuring in order to maintain his supremacy over the Party. This was Stalin's last Congress before his death.

The Twentieth Congress of the CPSU was held in February 1956 and Nikita Khrushchev was Stalin's successor, and he became the next General Secretary of the Party. Khrushchev addressed the Congress and made his famous several hour speech entitled 'On the Cult of Personality and its Consequences'. He spoke against the 'personality-cult' of Stalin and revealed the atrocities during his reign of power. He spoke in detail about the arrests and killings that occurred during the 'purges'. This was the beginning of the 'De-Stalinization'.

At the Twenty-first Congress of the CPSU held between January and February 1959, Khrushchev spoke on the progress of his plans to improve the economy. He continued to push his plans on the expansion of agricultural production through his cultivating 'virgin lands' policy. He also was improving industrial production by reforming and decentralizing the Soviet bureaucracy by giving more control to Regional Economic Councils. The Regional Economic Councils managed their own regional economies by developing local resources and industries. GOSPLAN was now responsible for general planning and coordination of resources and industrial production between the republics, as opposed to the total centralized control of the economy which was its previous responsibility.

The Twenty-second Congress of the CPSU was held between October and November 1961 and was the first to be held in the new Kremlin Palace of the Congresses. 'De-Stalinization' continued with the Congress voting to have Stalin's body removed from the mausoleum. Khrushchev's favour within the Party started to deteriorate during this time period. An agricultural crisis developed during the 'virgin lands' project, a consequence of a drought and improper cultivation methods. The Cuban missile crisis became an embarrassment for the USSR internationally. The decentralization of the Soviet bureaucracy to improve industrial production was not accepted by many of the Party's 'apparatchiks' (Party apparatus) as they felt their status and role within the Party was threatened. The Party's 'nomenklatura' (elite) also felt threatened by the continued 'De-Stalinization' as it was during the Stalin era that they gained prominence within the Party. The Party, specifically the members of the Presidium, removed Khrushchev from his position as General Secretary of the Party. This was his last Congress.

The Twenty-third Congress of the CPSU was held between March and April 1966 and Leonid Brezhnev was General Secretary of the Party. The Presidium was renamed the Politburo, a title used during the Stalin era. To re-centralize the Party, Brezhnev had Khrushchev's Regional Economic Councils abolished and the traditional Ministries that they had superseded restored. Economic reform of agriculture and industry was discussed. Agricultural reform consisted of a change in policy.

Left: Kremlin Palace of Congresses Pin, c. 1960s. **$5-$10**
The pin shows the backdrop that was used for the 22nd, 23rd and 24th Congresses of the CPSU. The Palace of Congresses in Moscow was built in 1961.

Right: Communist Party Pin, ca 1960s. **$5-$10**
Text: Our Party Leads Us Towards Communism!

Left: 23rd Congress of the CPSU Delegate Badge, c. 1966. **$85-$95**

Right: 23rd Congress of the CPSU Pin, c. 1966. **$5-$10**

Instead of the State buying fixed amounts of produce at fixed prices, the State would buy more produce at higher prices. Agriculture would focus on the centralized agricultural regions, improving canals, fertilizer and farm machinery, as opposed to the 'virgin lands' policy initiated by Krushchev. Industrial re-

Below: Communist Party Political Banner, c. 1960s. **$250-$350**
Velvet, 64" x 53".
Slogan on front: Under the Banner of Marxism-Leninism, Under the Leadership of the Communist Party – Forward, To the Victory of Communism!
Slogan on back: Workers of All Countries, Unite!

form would switch to a more supply and demand profitability economy. Brezhnev tightened the Party's reigns over society by using propaganda and censoring anti-Soviet literature.

The Twenty-fourth Congress of the CPSU was held in April 1971 during the 'détente' with the United States. The USSR had reached parity with the US in having a nuclear strategic launch force of equal size ending the U.S.'s nuclear superiority.

The Twenty-fifth Congress of the CPSU was held in February 1976. Brezhnev spoke of the success of the ninth Five-Year Plan as industry had an apparent growth in the output of

goods. Brezhnev stated that "Détente does not in any way rescind, nor can it rescind or alter, the laws of class struggle. We do not conceal the fact that we see in détente a path toward the creation of more favourable conditions for the peaceful construction of socialism and communism."

The Twenty-sixth Congress of the CPSU was held in February 1981 and it was Brezhnev's last. The guidelines for economic and social development of the USSR examined at the Congress stated, "The central objective of the eleventh Five-Year Plan is to ensure the further growth of the well-being of the Soviet people on the basis of the stable and consistent

Communist Party Political Banner, Velvet, 64" x 52", c. 1960s. **$250-$350**
Slogans on front -
Top: Workers of All Countries, Unite!
Bottom: Under the Banner of Marxism-Leninism,
Under the Leadership of the Communist Party – Forward, To the Victory of Communism!

Communist Party Political Banner, c. 1960s. **$250-$350**
Velvet, 52" x 45".
Slogan on back: Workers of All Countries, Unite!

Left: 24th Congress of the CPSU Delegate Badge, c. 1971. **$85-$95**

Right: 24th Congress of the CPSU Pins, c. 1971. **$5-$10**

Communist Party Political Banner, c. 1960s. **$165-$185**
Silk, 66" x 42 1/2".
Slogans on front -
Top left: Workers of All Countries, Unite!
Bottom: Under the Banner of Marxism-Leninism,
Under the Leadership of the Communist Party – Forward, to the Victory of
Communism!
Text on back: Glory Union of Soviet Socialist Republics!

Right: 25th Congress of the CPSU Delegate Badge, c. 1976. **$85-$95**

XXV Congress of the CPSU Banner, c. 1976. **$65-$85**
Silk, 38" x 32".
Text: Turn into Reality the Decisions of the XXV Congress of the CPSU.

Left: 25th Congress of the CPSU Pin Set, c. 1976. **$5-$10**

progress of the economy, the accelerated scientific and technological progress, the transition of the economy to the intensive road of development, the more rational utilization of the country's production potential, the utmost economization of all types of resources, and the improvement of the quality of work."

Leonid Brezhnev died on November 10, 1982. Between the Twenty-sixth and the Twenty-seventh Congresses the USSR lost two additional General Secretaries, Yuri Andropov who died in February 1984 and Konstantin Chernyenko who died in March 1985. In March 1985, an emergency plenum of the Central Committee was held and Mikhail Gorbachev became the new General Secretary of the Communist Party.

The Twenty-seventh Congress of the CPSU was held in February 1986. Mikhail Gorbachev was General Secretary and he announced radical changes that would have unrecoverable effects for the Party. The initiative called 'perestroika' (restructuring) was designed to restructure Party organizations and provide for a more democratic governmental process. The 'perestroika' would also be applied to improve the economy and would be used to break out of the stagnation the Soviet economy was enduring. In addition, the policy of 'glasnost' (openness) was introduced to improve the Communist Party's relationship with the citizens of the USSR and with foreign countries as well. Also at the Congress, a new programme was ratified announcing the complete destruction of nuclear weapons and other weapons of mass destruction by the end of the century.

The Twenty-eighth Congress of the CPSU was held in July 1990 and was its last. Gorbachev tried to consolidate his and the Party's control over the union. At the Congress there was continual infighting between the conservatives and the reformers of the Party membership. It was at this Congress that Boris Yeltsin unexpectedly went to the podium and said, "In connec-

Left: 25th Congress of the Communist Party of the Ukraine Pin Set, c. 1970s. **$5-$10**

Right: 26th Congress of the CPSU Delegate Badge, c. 1981. **$85-$95**

26th Congress of the CPSU Pin Set, c. 1981. **$5-$10**

XXVII Congress of the CPSU Table Medallion, c. 1986. **$45-$55**

Left: 27th Congress of the CPSU Delegate Badge, c. 1986. **$85-$95**

Right: 28th Congress of the CPSU Delegate Badge, c. 1990. **$85-$95**

tion with my appointment as Chairman of the Supreme Soviet of the RSFSR and my enormous responsibility to the people and to Russia, and considering the shift of society to a multiparty situation, I shall no longer be able to carry out only the decisions of the CPSU ... Therefore, in accordance with the

27th Congress of the CPSU Pin Set, c. 1986. **$5-$10**

responsibilities I have in the pre-election period, I am announcing my departure from the CPSU." After making this short speech he resigned from the Party. Yeltsin's denunciation of the Party resulted in a substantial increase in his popularity, and he now had control of the Russian Federation.

As a consequence of the policies of 'glasnost' (openness) and 'perestroika' (restructuring), the Soviet Union disintegrated during the Gorbachev era. The Russian Federation was under the leadership of Yeltsin and the other republics separated from the USSR and joined in the Confederation of Independent States (CIS). The Baltic States achieved their own independence and the Eastern block countries resigned from the Warsaw Pact. On December 25, 1991, Gorbachev resigned as General Secretary of the Communist Party as its usefulness was no more. Shortly thereafter on December 31, 1991, the large red flag with the gold hammer and sickle of the USSR was replaced with the red, white and blue flag of the new Russia on the top of the Kremlin tower. The world's first socialist state, the USSR, did not exist anymore.

This page:
Communist Party Plenum Delegate Badges.
1. 60th Year of the October Revolution 1977. **$85-$95**
Text on front: 60 Years On Lenin's Path.
2. 70th Year of the October Revolution 1987. **$85-$95**
Text on front: 70 Years of the Great October.
3. 50th Year of the USSR 1972. **$85-$95**
Text on back: 50th Year of the Formation of the Union SSR (Union of Soviet Socialist Republics) Moscow. Kremlin December 1972.
4. 60th Year of the USSR 1982. **$85-$95**
Text on back: 60th Year of the USSR Moscow . Kremlin 1982.

50 Years in the Communist Party Award Badge. **$35-$45**

XIX All-Union Party Conference Pin, c. 1988. **$5-$10**

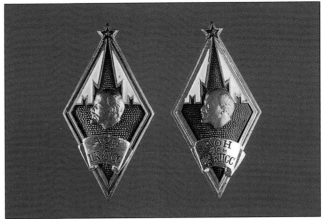

The University of Marxism-Leninism (UML) Graduation Badges.
1. 11 Republics Coat-of-Arms, c. 1937-1947. **$25-$35**
2. 15 Republics Coat-of-Arms, 2 variants, c. 1960s. **$20-$25**
The University of Marxism-Leninism was the highest communist political school in the Soviet Union and was necessary for citizens with political aspirations.

Social Sciences Academy (AON) Under the Central Committee of the CPSU (TsK KPSS) Graduation Badges, c. 1960s-1980s (2 versions). **$20-$25**
This was a Communist party school for party officials overseeing the arts and culture.

FOUR

SOVIET SECURITY FORCES

Shortly after the revolution and the establishment of the Bolsheviks to power there was a growing opposition building within the newly established Soviet Republic. Lenin became aware of the growing 'counterrevolutionary' forces which were a threat to the Bolshevik regime. He came to the conclusion that "a special system of organized violence" would be necessary to establish the 'dictatorship of the proletariat'.

The Soviet security force was created on December 20, 1917, about a month and a half after the Bolshevik revolution. The ancestor of the well-known KGB was the Cheka, which was the acronym for 'Extraordinary Commission to Fight the Counterrevolution and Sabotage'. Lenin selected as the Cheka's first leader Felix Dzerzhinskii a professional revolutionary from Poland.

Upon the creation of the Cheka the Council of Peoples Commissars (Sovnarkom) approved a policy to deal with the counterrevolutionaries. It stated that the seizure of property, resettlement, the depriving of ration cards, publication of lists of enemies of the people, etc. would be used as necessary to deal with the problem.

The Bolsheviks were victorious in overthrowing the unpopular Provisional Government but still had a minority of support throughout the country. Lenin approved elections to the Constituent Assembly after the revolution in order to establish social democracy. The Social Revolutionaries (SR's) the Bolshevik's main rival on the left received the majority of the vote in the election, while the Bolsheviks received approximately one-quarter of the vote. When the Constituent Assembly convened in January 1918, Lenin and the Bolsheviks broke it up stating it was 'counterrevolutionary'. Lenin realized that

the Cheka would have to be used to deal with the 'counterrevolutionary' forces that were growing within the country.

On August 30, 1918, after speaking to the workers at the Michelson works in Moscow, Lenin was shot and seriously wounded by a Social Revolutionary activist named Fanya Kaplan. After this incident the Cheka unleashed its suppression against the 'counterrevolutionary' forces and it became known as the 'Red Terror'. Dzerzhinskii made a statement about the Cheka that August, "We represent in ourselves organized terror, this must be said very clearly."

The Cheka was originally established as a temporary department eventually to be abolished once the Bolshevik regime was firmly in power. By the early part of 1920, the 'counterrevolutionary' forces were approaching defeat and did not pose a serious threat to the Bolshevik regime. The Civil War was entering into its final stages with a Bolshevik victory at hand. On January 17, 1920, Lenin and Dzerzhinskii signed a decree announcing the end of the death penalty for enemies of the Soviet authorities.

By the year 1921, the Civil War ended with a Bolshevik victory and the threat of domestic and foreign 'counterrevolutionary' forces declined. It was at this point that the Bolsheviks decided that the Cheka was not required anymore. On February 6, 1922, the Cheka was replaced by the State Political Directorate (GPU), which became part of and subordinate to the newly formed Peoples Commissariat for Internal Affairs (NKVD). Initially the powers of the GPU were drastically reduced when compared to that of its predecessor the Cheka. But by May of that year Lenin stated, "The law should not abolish terror; to promise that would be self-delusion or deception…" Decrees passed in August and October, 1922, gave the GPU powers to exile, imprison, and if necessary execute counter-revolutionaries and criminals.

On December 30, 1922, the Union of Soviet Socialist Republics (USSR) was formed. In the following year the NKVD was abolished and the GPU became a federal agency called the Unified State Political Directorate (OGPU) with ever increasing powers. The OGPU had judicial powers attached to it and used them when trying counterrevolutionaries, spies, and terrorists. It was a nationwide organization which also had additional duties such as the administration of the network of labour camps (GULAG). The OGPU and its successors were firmly established at the center of the Soviet State.

Lenin died on January 21, 1924, and almost immediately thereafter Joseph Stalin started pursuing his quest for power within the Party. A little over two years later on July 20, 1926, Felix Dzerzhinskii died of a heart attack, also helping Stalin in his quest for ultimate power within the Party. Dzerzhinskii was the chairman of the OGPU and also of the Supreme Economic Council during the New Economic Policy (NEP) which was endorsed by Lenin. Dzerzhinskii would have opposed the attacks on the 'bourgeois specialists' in industry which were helping revive the nation's economy after the perilous Civil War. After his death the 'bourgeois specialists' stated, "What a shame Dzerzhinskii's gone. It was easy to work with him. He appreciated and defended us specialists." He would have also opposed the brutal class war against the peasants in the countryside that Stalin was to launch within the next few years. With Dzerzhinskii gone, Stalin's rise to power was becoming more assured.

Vyacheslav Menzhinsky became the next leader of the OGPU. He was an intellectual individual but did not have the powerful stature and charisma as did Dzerzhinskii.

By 1927, it was members of the Bolshevik Party itself that were opposing Stalin's rise to power. Stalin started using the OGPU to strengthen his own personal authority within the Bolshevik Party. Under Stalin, the OGPU started to use infiltration techniques usually used against counterrevolutionaries and opponents to the Party. In the past, the Cheka was established to combat the counterrevolution, under Stalin, the OGPU was used to combat opposition to Stalin, even from within the Party itself.

In 1928, the first Five-Year Plan was introduced by Stalin to embark on a massive programme of industrialization and forced collectivization of the peasants and Kulaks in the countryside. The Five-Year Plan was created to transform Russia's primitive agriculturally based economy into a large industrial-

Medal for the 50th Anniversary of the Soviet Militia. **$25-$45**
Instituted November 20, 1967 and over 250,000 were issued.
Text on back: For the Commemoration of the Fiftieth Anniversary of the Soviet Militia 1917-1967.

ized economy. The collectivization was also designed to eliminate the Kulaks, the better-off peasants as a class. The Soviet authorities under Stalin's rule considered the better-off peasants as enemies of the revolution because of their bourgeois mentality. The massive industrialization was designed to create a fully socialized economy in the USSR. The New Economic Policy (NEP) which was created by Lenin to revive the ailing Soviet economy after the Civil War, was officially put to an end by Stalin in December 1929.

In the Soviet Union during the 1930s, Stalin used imaginary conspiracies as an excuse to justify the slaughter of millions of people labeled 'enemies of the people'. Using the OGPU, a determined onslaught against the Kulaks and the bourgeois specialists in industry began. Stalin stated that the Kulaks were "the sworn enemies of the collective farm movement". It was the OGPU that rounded up entire Kulak families by the thousands, marched them off to railway stations and transported them to the Siberian wilderness to fend for themselves. The remaining peasants that were left behind were put into collective farms (Kolkhozes) under the forced collectivization. The OGPU set up a network of labour camps (GULAG) using prisoners as a major source of labour for the Soviet economy.

After Menzhinsky's death in May 1934, Genrikh Yagoda became the head of the OGPU. He was loyal to Stalin which enabled him to further his career within the security forces. He was an uncultured brutal individual. In July 1934, the OGPU was changed to become the Main Administration of State Security (GUGB) and became part of and subordinate to the re-established Peoples Commissariat for Internal Affairs (NKVD). The regular police, political police, criminal investigation, internal troops, border troops and the entire penal system was combined into this one powerful organization that answered directly to Stalin himself.

By the mid-1930s, Stalin became more concerned about the opposition to his leadership. The era known as the 'purges' of the 1930s began. Stalin started the assault against the Party membership that he felt were actual or potential adversaries to his leadership. The assassination in 1934 of Leningrad Party Chief Sergei Kirov signaled the beginning of the 'Great Terror'. Kirov the politician was gaining favour among the Soviet people and with members of the Party and Stalin saw him as a rival. To counter this, Stalin covertly had Kirov assassinated and the death was blamed as a 'counterrevolutionary' conspiracy. It became the justification for the 'purges'. Trotskyites, Zinovievites, members of the Workers' Opposition, etc. were blamed for Kirov's assassination. The purge of Party members started in 1933 and continued in earnest to 1938.

In 1936, Nikolai Yezhov became the successor to Yagoda as head of the NKVD. In the summer of 1936 on Stalin's initiative, the Central Committee passed a secret resolution which gave the NKVD extraordinary powers to destroy all 'enemies of the people'. Under Yezhov all restraints that had hindered the liquidation of Stalin's imaginary enemies were removed. The years 1936 to 1938 were the years at the height of the 'Great Terror' and Yezhov presided over it.

Rather than defending the revolution, the NKVD's main purpose under Stalin was to combat the imaginary 'enemies of the people' which Stalin feared as they opposed him. People that worked in important institutions such as the Red Army, the Communist Party, and even the NKVD itself, were being victimized by the 'purges'. The 'purges' took a devastating toll on the original Bolsheviks, as Stalin wanted to liquidate them in order to secure his power and supremacy within the Party. Eighty percent of the members of the Central Committee elected in 1934 were shot or imprisoned. All but three percent of the delegates at the next Congress in 1939 were absent. Seventy-five of the eighty members of the Supreme Military Council were shot. More than half of the Red Army military officers were executed. Within the NKVD itself its hierarchy was purged twice. Nineteen million people of the USSR were arrested during the 'purges' and at least seven million were shot or died in the GULAG. All this was done because of Stalin's growing paranoia against the Soviet leadership and the people that he thought were against him. His intent was to have a Party of

Honoured Member of the NKVD Award Badge, c. 1930s-1940s. **$350-$550**

virgin membership which would be totally subordinate to him to secure his power base. The 'purges' were not against the counterrevolution but were against the government and the people of the country, the imaginary 'enemies of the people'.

On December 8, 1938, Lavrenti Beria previously head of the Transcaucasian NKVD became the new head of the NKVD replacing Yezhov. In February 1941, the GUGB which was part of the NKVD and responsible for state security, was removed from the NKVD and became an independent Commissariat called the Peoples Commissariat for State Security (NKGB). This only lasted a few months as the GUGB became part of the NKVD again. During the years leading to the Soviet Union's participation in the 'Great Patriotic War', the NKVD was conducting a more selective terror within the country. Trotskyites, senior officials of the NKVD, and hundreds of high-ranking military specialists and officers were being interrogated and put to death.

During the war the NKVD had approximately three-quarter of a million troops in divisions and brigades. This did not include the numerous other independent units and Border Troops. The NKVD also had 'special departments' known as the 'Smersh' ('Smersh' was an acronym in Russian for "Death to Spies."). The 'Smersh' was created in 1943 providing counter-intelligence within the armed forces. The 'Smersh' was responsible during the war to uncover spies, saboteurs and subversives within the military. The 'Smersh' were also used as blocking detachments which were behind the regular forces to prevent retreat. If a soldier was caught retreating from the front lines during battle he would be shot dead by the 'Smersh' and this drastic measure was used as a deterrent to cowardice.

In April 1943, the GUGB was removed from the NKVD and became the NKGB an independent Commissariat again.

In March 1946, the NKVD and the NKGB were raised in status from Commissariats to Ministries. The NKVD was now called the Ministry of Internal Affairs (MVD) and the NKGB became the Ministry of State Security (MGB). Beria's vast security empire grew immensely during the war. By the end of the war Stalin was concerned about the immense power Beria had accrued. As a result of Stalin's concern, in 1946, Sergei Kruglov, Beria's former first deputy became the head of the MVD, while Viktor Abakumov who was head of the 'Smersh' during the war became the head of the MGB. Beria was removed from these Ministries and became a member of the Politburo and deputy Chairman of the Council of Ministers.

When the war ended the power of the MGB encompassed the satellite states of Eastern Europe. The MGB had power over the satellite states' police forces and infiltrated and broke-up anti-communist, anti-Soviet, or any other independent groups opposing the regime.

During the last years of Stalin's life he became increasingly paranoid and physically weak. During the winter of 1952-1953, Stalin was preparing to start another 'purge'. In January 1953, he ordered the arrest of many doctors, mostly Jews, on charges of medical assassinations. This was the so-called 'doctors plot'. As with the assassination of Sergei Kirov in 1934, the medical assassinations would be blamed as a 'counterrevolutionary' conspiracy used as an excuse for another 'purge' of the Party membership to secure his power over the Party. Also during this time, Beria discovered that Stalin was planning to remove him. On the night of March 1-2, 1953, Stalin suffered a stroke and Beria was already making plans to succeed him. During Stalin's final hours Beria had a concealed hatred for him. When Stalin was conscious, Beria kissed his hands. When Stalin relapsed into unconsciousness, he would spit at him. Khrushchev and the other members of the Presidium witnessed his abhorrent behavior. On March 5, 1953, Stalin died and Beria was exultant. Within a day after Stalin's death Beria amalgamated the MGB and the MVD into an enlarged MVD organization entirely under his command.

Nikita Krushchev and the other members of the Presidium of the Communist Party were making plans to overthrow Beria. On June 26, 1954, the Presidium met for a special meeting and Beria was called to attend. Khrushchev rose from his seat and opened the meeting by saying, "There is one item on the agenda: the anti-party, divisive activity of imperialist agent Beria. This is a proposal to drop him from the Presidium and from the Central Committee, expel him from the Party, and hand him over to the court martial. Who is in favour?" All of the members of the Presidium were in favour of expelling him from the

Honoured Member of the MVD Award Badge, c. 1960s-1980s. **$250-$350**

Below:
Excellent Border Guard Award Badges, c. 1950s.
1. Initial version, 4-piece construction. **$85-$95**
2. Final version, 1-piece construction. **$55-$75**

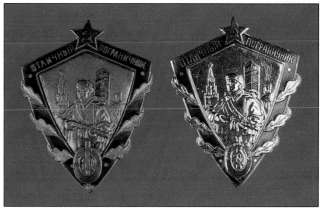

Party and hand him over to the court martial. Shortly thereafter a group of army officers arrested Beria and took him away. Beria became the third chief of the NKVD to be executed following Yagoda and Yezhov in the 1930s.

In March 1954, the Soviet security forces were reorganized for the last time. The Communist Party under the leadership of Khrushchev, demoted the MGB from a Ministry to a Committee and was under the auspices of the Council of Ministers to keep it under political control. The MGB became known as the familiar Committee for State Security (KGB). By the mid-1960s, the KGB became firmly established as the Communist Party's organ of social and political control of the State. Also in 1954, the Ministry of Internal Affairs (MVD) was created as a separate organization. The Border Guard Troops were initially under the control of the NKVD/MVD until March 1957, when they then became part of the KGB.

During Khrushchev's policies of reorganizing and decentralizing the State apparatus, the MVD was transformed into the Ministry for Maintaining Public Order (MOOP). In February 1962, the MOOP was created and was divided into fifteen divisions, one in each of the fifteen republics of the USSR. In

July 1966, as a consequence of Brezhnev's re-centralization policies, the fifteen divisions of the MOOP were amalgamated into the All-Union MOOP. In November 1968, the MOOP was transformed back into its original form as the MVD.

By 1964, Khrushchev was losing favour with members of the Presidium of the Communist Party. The Cuban missile crisis of 1962 was considered a humiliation to Soviet authorities. A poor harvest in 1963 caused the Soviet Union to buy much needed grain from the West. Also, Khrushchev was continually reorganizing and decentralizing the Party and State apparatus in an attempt to improve the economy which caused a large discontentment among members of the Party and thousands of apparatchiks. The Presidium was deciding to overthrow him by arresting him but decided against it. Instead they used evidence of his role during Stalin's 'purges' in the Ukraine in the mid-1930s. Khrushchev accepting his fate quietly resigned as General Secretary of the Party.

In October 1964 after Khrushchev's removal, Leonid Brezhnev became the next General Secretary of the Communist Party of the Soviet Union (CPSU). Under Brezhnev the 1960s was a decade of stability, while the 1970s became known as the years of stagnation.

In 1967, Brezhnev named Yuri Andropov as head of the KGB. Since 1957, Andropov was head of the Central Committee Department for Relations with Communist and Workers' Parties of Socialist Countries. Brezhnev stated that he wanted Andropov "to bring the KGB closer to the Central Committee." Andropov was the first senior Party official to become the head of the KGB and at the same time held a seat on the Politburo. Brezhnev wanted the Communist Party itself to have control over the affairs of the KGB. After being Chairman of the KGB for fifteen years, Andropov became General Secretary of the Communist Party of the Soviet Union (CPSU) after Brezhnev's death in 1982.

The massive secret police organization of the KGB was the Party's security watchdog maintaining social and political control over the State. The KGB employed for domestic surveillance an estimated 700,000 agents throughout the country. One in every 250 adult Soviet citizens worked in some capacity as an informant for the KGB. Many of its employees worked in the personnel departments of factories, government agencies, and educational institutions. Full-time agents were supplemented by tens of thousands of casual workers paid by the KGB as informers. In a residential apartment building for example, residents took it for granted that the little old lady that ran the elevator was a KGB informer paid to report on suspicious events such as a visit by a foreigner.

KGB Border Guard Award Banner, c. 1950s. **$1250-$1450**
Velvet, 64" x 50".
Text on front: To the Best Collective for Military-Patronage Work from the Border Guards of the Leningrad District.
Slogan on back: For Our Soviet Homeland.

Left: Excellent Service in the Internal Army for the Ministry of Maintaining Public Order (VVMOOP) Award Badge, c. 1962-1968. **$45-$55**

Right: Excellent Policeman for the Ministry of Maintaining Public Order (MOOP) Award Badge, c. 1962-1968. **$45-$55**

Original Issue Honourary Member of the KGB Award Badges.
1. 50th Year 1917 1967. **$115-$170**
2. 70th Year 1917 1987. **$115-$170**

Left: 50th Year KGB Award Badge, c. 1967. **$45-$65**

Right: Honoured Member of the KGB Award Badge, c. 1980s. **$45-$65**

Above:
Medals for Irreproachable Service in the KGB of the USSR.
Instituted September 14, 1957.
1. 10 years. **$25-$45**
2. 15 years. **$25-$45**
3. 20 years. **$25-$45**

Left:
KGB Merit Badges, c. 1970s-1980s.
1. 1st class. **$30-$45**
2. 2nd class. **$30-$45**

The KGB was the largest secret police and espionage organization in the world. Its main function after the 'Great Patriotic War' was to maintain the Soviet Union's influence in Eastern Europe and in other parts of the world. It also had to deal with the 'Cold War' that developed between the USSR and its 'main adversary' the United States. The KGB's foreign functions were espionage and conducting covert operations aimed at strengthening Soviet power and influence. The KGB organization had approximately three-quarter of a million employees of which, 90,000 were officers, 240,000 were Border

KGB USSR Officer on Duty Badge, c. 1970s-1980s. **$45-$55**

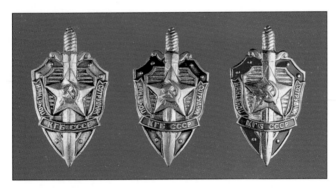

Honourary Member of the KGB Award Badges, c. 1980s.
Late issue and replacement copies. **$25-$35**

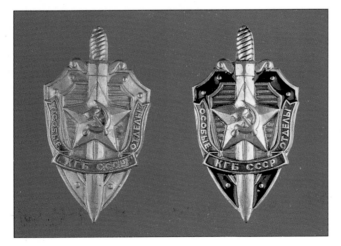

Honourary Member of the KGB 'Special Department' (counterintelligence) Award Badges, c. 1980s. **$25-$35**
Late issue and replacement copies.

KGB Internal Security Sleeve Insignia.
1. Standard. **$10-$15**
2. USSR variation. **$10-$15**

Guards and internal security troops, and the rest were support staff. The Border Guard's Chief Directorate of the KGB was equipped with armour, artillery and navy coast guard vessels.

The MVD maintained law and order within the country. It controlled the Militia (Civil Police Force), GAI (State Automobile Inspectorate) and the fire departments. The MVD had 260,000 internal troops, which roles were to guard important State installations and to maintain control of the State's labour camps (GULAG). The internal troops were equipped with armoured vehicles and tanks.

In the mid-1980s under the leadership of Mikhail Gorbachev, political reforms were emerging under 'glasnost' (openness) and 'perestroika' (restructuring) in the USSR. The days were becoming numbered for the future of the KGB. When the Soviet Union dissolved on December 26, 1991, the KGB and its counterpart the MVD were no more.

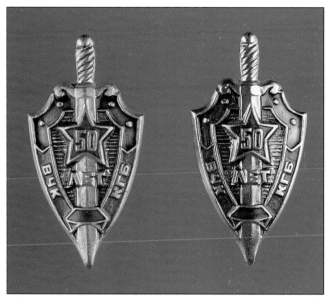

50th Year of the KGB Award Badges, c. 1980s.
Late issue and replacement copies.
1. Officers. **$15-$25**
2. NCO. **$15-$25**

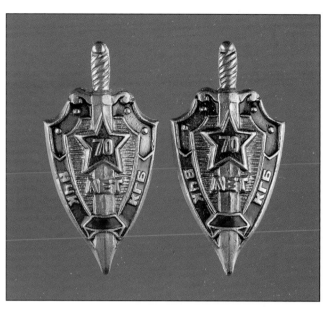

70th Year of the KGB Award Badges, c. 1980s.
Late issue and replacement copies.
1. Officers. **$15-$25**
2. NCO. **$15-$25**

KGB Border Guard Award Badges.
1. 50th Year. c. 1968. **$65-$86**
2. 60th Year. c. 1978. **$65-$85**
3. 70th Year. c. 1988. **$55-$75**
4. 75th Year. c. 1993 (Soviet Style/Post Soviet Era). **$45-$65**

Award Certificate for the "60th Year of the Border Guard Troops of the KGB", c. 1978. **$45-$55**

Text on top: CERTIFICATE

Middle: By the Order of the Commander of the Border Guard Troops of the KGB

Under the SM (Council of Ministers) USSR Awards the Badge "60 Years of the Border Guard Troops of the KGB".

Bottom: Commander of the Border Guard Troops Under the SM (Council of Ministers) USSR General-Colonel (Matrosov).

Medal for Guarding the State Border of the USSR. **$95-$115**

Awarded to Border Guard Troops, Personnel of the Soviet Armed Forces and civilians for defending the USSR's State Border. Instituted July 13, 1950 and over 55,000 were issued.

Text on back: For Distinguished Service in Guarding the State Border of the USSR.

Excellent Border Guard Award Badge, c. 1960s. **$35-$45**

Left and below:
Excellent Border Guard Award Badges, c. 1970s-1980s.
1. 2nd class. **$25-$45**
2. 1st class. **$25-$45**

Senior Border Guard Badges, c. 1970s-1980s.
1. 1st class. **$25-$35**
2. 2nd class. **$25-$35**

Excellent Border Guard Award Document with Felix Dzerzhinskii's Portrait (unissued), c. 1970s-1980s. **$10-$15**
Text: For Our Soviet Homeland!
AWARD DOCUMENT

KGB Border Guard Sleeve Insignia. **$10-$15**

Left: Excellent Policeman of the MVD USSR Award Badge, c. 1950s.
Note: 16 Republic Coat-of-Arms (1948-1956).

Right: Excellent Service in the MVD Award Badge, c. 1970s-1980s. **$45-$55**

Excellent Policeman of the MVD Award Badges.
1. 1st Class, c. 1970s. **$25-$35**
2. 2nd Class, c. 1980s. **$25-$35**

Excellent Policeman of the MVD Award Certificate (unissued), c. 1980s. **$5-$10**
Text on top: Ministry of Internal Affairs USSR CERTIFICATE
Text on bottom: Rewards the Badge for "Excellent Policeman"

Left: Meritorious (Local) Police Station Inspector Award Badge, c. 1970s-1980s. **$45-$55**

Right: MVD USSR Chief Guard of the Internal Army Breast Badge, c. 1970s-1980s. **$45-$65**

Medals for Irreproachable Service in the MVD of the USSR. Instituted September 14, 1957.
1. 10 years. **$25-$45**
2. 15 years. **$25-$45**
3. 20 years. **$25-$45**

Internal Army of the MVD (VVMVD) Merit Badges, c. 1970s-1980s.
1. 1st class. **$20-$30**
2. 2nd class. **$20-$30**

MVD Specialist Badges, c. 1960s-1970s.
1. 1st class. **$20-$30**
2. 2nd class. **$20-$30**
3. 3rd class. **$20-$30**

Right:
MVD Specialist Badges, c. 1978 issue.
1. 1st class. **$20-$30**
2. 2nd class. **$20-$30**
3. 3rd class. **$20-$30**

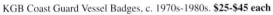

Left: XXV Congress of the CPSU (PSKR) Coast Guard Vessel Commemorative Badge, c. 1976. **$25-$35**

Right: XX Years of the Coast Guard Vessel 'Dzerzhinskii' Commemorative Badge. **$25-$35**

Left: XX Years of the Kirov (KPSKR) Coast Guard Vessel Commemorative Badge. **$25-$35**

Right: KGB Coast Guard Vessel Pin, c. 1970s-1980s. **$10-$15**

KGB Coast Guard Vessel Badges, c. 1970s-1980s. **$25-$45 each**
1. In the Name of the XXV Congress of the CPSU.
2. In the Name of the XXVI Congress of the CPSU.
3. In the Name of the 27th Congress of the CPSU.
4. In the Name of the 70th Year of the 'Cheka – KGB'.
5. Coast Guard Vessel.
6. 'Volga' (PSKR) Coast Guard Vessel.
7. 'Kamchatka' Coast Guard Vessel.
8. 'Sakhalin' Coast Guard Vessel.

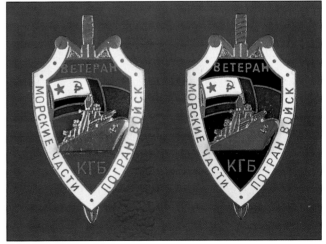

Veteran of the KGB Naval Units of the Border Guard Troops Award Badges, c. 1970s-1980s. **$25-$45**

Left: Higher Military Navy Border Guard Academy (BBMPU) NKVD KGB Graduation Badge, c. 1970s-1980s. **$25-$45**

KGB Coast Guard Naval Flag, bunting. **$65-$155**

KGB Coast Guard Supreme Commander (Chairman of the KGB) Flag, bunting. **$65-$155**

KGB Academy Graduation Badges (two variations), c. 1970s-1980s. **$25-$45**

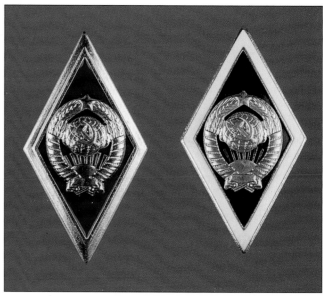

MVD Militia Academy Graduation Badges, c. 1970s-1980s.
1. Highest MVD Academy. **$25-$45**
2. MVD Academy. **$25-$45**

Far left: MVD Academy Graduation Badge, c. 1970s-1980s. **$25-$45**

Left: MVD USSR 'Highest Courses' Graduation Badge, c. 1970s-1980s. **$25-$45**

Military Political Academy (VPU) of the MVD USSR Graduation Badges, c. 1970s-1980s. The blue badges designate intermediate level courses and the white badges are for the highest level courses. **$25-$45**

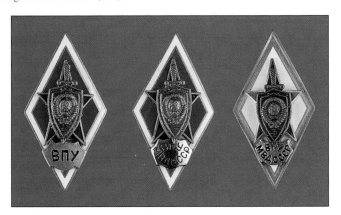

Left: MVD Political and Propaganda Academy Graduation Badge, c. 1970s-1980s. **$25-$45**

Right: Tomsky Special Militia Academy (TSSShM) Graduation Badge, c. 1970s-1980s. **$25-$45**

Tomsky Special Militia Academy (TSSShM) Anniversary Badges.
1. 30th Year. **$25-$35**
2. 40th Year. **$25-$35**

Left: 12th Graduation Class of the 'OMSKY' MVD Academy. **$25-$45**

Right: S.M. Kirov Border Guard Troops 1940-1980 Badge. **$25-$35**

Left: 'LPTU' MVD Academy Graduation Badge, c. 1950s-1960s. **$35-$55**

Right: The Leningrad Department of Fire Protection Academy Graduation Badge. **$25-$35**

50th Year of the MVD USSR Academy Commemorative Pin. **$15-$25**

Above and below:
MVD Specialists Badges,
c. 1970s-1980s.
1. 1st class Tutor. **$20-$30**
2. 1st class Specialist. **$20-$30**
3. 2nd class Specialist. **$20-$30**

"Dynamo" Organization Pennant. Silk, 22" x 13". **$25-$35**
Text: All-Union Physical Culture-Sports Order of Lenin Organization "Dynamo".
Note: The "Dynamo" Organization was the athletic organization of the Soviet Security Forces.

FIVE

COMMUNISM AND SOVIET LABOUR

Communism

It was Karl Marx and Friedrich Engels, both German political philosophers and revolutionaries that founded and developed the theories of socialism, which in its ultimate form is known as Communism. Both men had independently studied and developed their theories about socialism and it wasn't until 1844 that Engels met Marx for the first time in Paris. They soon discovered that their theories were very much identical.

In 1845, Marx was ordered to leave Paris because of his revolutionary activities and he eventually settled in Brussels. In Brussels, he began organizing and directing a network of revolutionary groups called Communist Correspondence Committees in many cities throughout Europe. In 1847, these committees were amalgamated to form the Communist League. Marx and Engels formulated a statement of principles for the Communist League and wrote the famous article the Communist Manifesto. It was the first statement on the principals of modern socialist doctrine and was written by Marx partly on the basis of a draft written by Engels.

In the Communist Manifesto, Marx states that capitalism would eventually develop into a confrontation between the ruling Bourgeoisie (the capitalist) and the oppressed Proletariat (the working class). As a consequence of the desire of the capitalist to continually increase profits, the working class would increase in size, so that it could provide the required increase in economic production in the factories. The bourgeois with their increasing wealth became the powerful few in society, living off of the labour of the numerous proletariat. Due to the low wages and miserable lifestyle of the large numbers of poor working class people in society, they eventually would revolt

Manifesto of the Communist Party by K. Marx and F. Engels. **$10-$15**
Progress Publishers Moscow, c. 1969.
Text on back: K. Marx and F. Engels, Manifesto of the Communist Party, In the English Language.

against their oppressors. After a successful revolution, the factories would be run 'by the people-for the people', doing away with private ownership and a classless society would develop. The factories would produce what the people needed instead of producing goods strictly for profit.

In the Communist Manifesto the famous slogan, 'Workers of all countries, unite!' and in a later work, 'Dictatorship of the Proletariat' were written. Both became slogans for Communism in the USSR and were seen on banners, orders, pins, and badges during the Soviet era.

Karl Marx died in 1883. After his death his socialist doctrines were revived by Vladimir Ilyich Lenin, who developed and applied them in Russia. Marxism became the core of the theory and practice of Bolshevism. The State exercised con-

K. Marx. F. Engels. V. Lenin 1924
Bronze Table Medallion. **$80-$95**
Text on back: Lenin in Moscow.

Right: Marx/Lenin Pins, c. 1970s-
1980s. **$5-$10**

Marx/Lenin Labour Award Banner, c. 1970s. **$95-$135**
Silk, 57" x 32 1/2".
Slogans on front -
Top left: Workers of all Countries, Unite!
Bottom: Challenge Banner for Achieving High Marks in a Socialist Competition.
Slogan on back: "We Will Come to the Victory of Communist Labour!" V.I.
Lenin

trol over the measure of labour and consumption according to the socialist principle, 'From each according to his ability, to each according to his work.'

Soviet Labour

Russia at the time of the Bolshevik revolution had essentially an agriculturally based economy and was not as industrialized as the nations of the West. After the Civil War during the latter part of the 1920s, the Soviet government concentrated their efforts on developing heavy industry to strengthen the country.

In order to create a modern socialist economy, the peasants primitive and inefficient methods of agriculture had to be transformed to provide the necessary food products for the large industrialized cities. At the same time, industry would have to be developed to provide the machinery and consumer goods to provide an incentive for the peasants to grow more produce. Unfortunately, neither of these economic requirements existed at that time. To overcome this obstacle and speed up the development of a large modern socialist economy Stalin introduced the Five-Year Plan, which was a centralized economic plan for the country.

In 1928, Stalin ushered in the first Five-Year Plan (1928-1932) and its main goal was the development of heavy industry such as steel-making, mining and the manufacturing of machine tools. In December 1929, a meeting of high-output piece workers called 'shockworkers' made a proclamation call-

ing for the first Five-Year Plan quotas to be completed in four years. 'Five in Four' became a slogan during that time. During the 'shockworkers' movement, incentives in the form of awards and honourary titles were given along with material benefits such as larger ration cards and better apartments to increase productivity. During the first Five-Year Plan large-scale industrial development doubled.

During the second Five-Year Plan (1933-1937), the Soviet Union became one of the largest steel producing nations in the world. Prior to the advent of the 'Great Patriotic War' (World War II), the USSR was number one in the world in the mining of manganese ore and in the production of synthetic rubber; number two in the world in oil production, the manufacture of machine tools and tractors; number three in the world in electric power generation, steel, cast iron and aluminum production; number four in the world in the production of coal and cement. At that time the USSR accounted for ten percent

'Udarnik' Shockworker of the First Five-Year Plan Award Badge, c. 1930s. **$220-$235**

'Udarnik' Shockworker 1932 at the Completion of the Five-Year Plan Award Badge, c. 1932. Issued during the XV Anniversary of the October Revolution 1917-1932. **$180-$215**

'Udarnik' Shockworker Fulfilling the VI (six) Directives of Stalin Award Badge, c. 1930s. **$180-$215**

of the world's industrial output. The Soviet Union's annual industrial growth rate from the late 1930s to the early 1950s was at an astonishing twelve to thirteen percent which was exceptional compared to other industrialized nations of that period. As a result of the many Five-Year Plans that followed with the use of the nation's labour force, the Soviet Union was transformed from a peasant based economy into a modern industrial state and eventually a superpower.

The Communist Party in conjunction with the trade unions were the main bodies of Soviet labour policy after 1928, when the NEP was abolished during the Stalin era. The leadership of the Trade Unions Council were prominent figures within the Party. The trade unions carried out the policies and economic objectives of the Party within the factories. The trade unions initial function after the revolution was to promote the welfare of the workers within the factories but eventually became instruments of the Party being more concerned with labour productivity. This situation was exasperated during the initial Five-Year Plans of forced industrialization. Workers in the factories were forbidden to strike as strikes were considered detrimental to the 'workers' State'.

There was a heavy labour turnover rate in the 1930s, which was becoming detrimental to productivity as workers were continually looking for better working conditions and housing. To combat this, the anti-worker legislation of 1940 resulted in fines or imprisonment for unauthorized job changes or absenteeism. Each worker had to carry a worker's logbook which

was kept by the management of the factory at which they worked. This prevented unauthorized movements of workers from one factory to another. On April 25, 1956, this legislation was repealed and the Soviet worker's rights to change jobs was restored.

The first Five-Year Plan (1928-1932) also concentrated on the collectivization of agriculture. The Soviet State used the collective farms as an effective way of ensuring quotas of food products for the city populations in order to facilitate the rapid industrialization. During the 1930s, many of the better-off peasants called Kulaks opposed the collectivization of their farms. Hundreds of thousands were either shot or deported to Siberia or other remote areas of the USSR as punishment for not obeying Soviet authorities.

There were two types of collective farms established during the 1930s. The Sovkhozes (State farms) were operated by the State and the farmers were employed by the State. In the Kolkhozes (collective farms) the land was socialized but parts of the land on a farm was allocated to individual families for private use. In order for the State to maintain control over the Kolkhozes, State-run Machine and Tractor Stations (MTS) were established by a decree of June 5, 1929. Farm machinery and personnel from the MTS's were used at the Kolkhozes. In return for the MTS's services, the State received its required allotment of produce. In February 1958, Khrushchev abolished the MTS's as he believed it would be more efficient to have the farmers themselves operate the machinery on their farms.

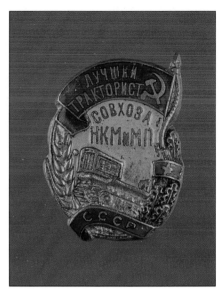

'Udarnik' Shockworker of a Collective Farm (Kolkhoz) Award Badge, c. 1930s. **$175-$205** *Text*: The Collective Farmer is the Firm Supporter of Soviet Power in the Countryside.

Excellence in a Socialist Competition on an Agricultural Farm Ministry of Supply of the Harvest Award Badge, c. 1940s. **$85-$95**

Best Tractor Driver of a Sovkhoz (State farm), c. 1940s. **$85-$95**

The forced collectivization of the peasants was not a success as agriculture productivity actually declined and never reached the pre-collectivization levels right through to the 1950s. Khrushchev in the early 1950s, recognized that Soviet agriculture had failed to meet the food demands of the nation of the USSR. On Khrushchev's 'virgin lands' initiative, a massive campaign of cultivating tens of millions of hectares of virgin and fallow lands in Kazakhstan, Siberia and the Urals was embarked in the mid 1950s. By 1956, 33 million hectares of land had been cleared and cultivated. Increasing the use of modern equipment and mechanization during the 'virgin lands' initiative, grain production rose substantially during the decade from 1956 to 1966.

Thousands of Soviet youth from the Komsomol participated in the cultivation of the 'virgin lands'. At the beginning of the 'virgin lands' proposal in 1954 Khrushchev stated, "Let's appeal to our Soviet youth, to our Communist Youth League. I'm sure that hundreds of thousands of young people will respond if it's a matter of providing our country with grain." At that time many Komsomol youth gathered at the main hall of the Supreme Soviet at the Kremlin to show their support for the initiative.

In order to encourage the production of goods in the factories and on the farms, incentives were developed by the Soviet government. At the end of 1917, Lenin wrote an article called, "How to organize competition?" During the first Five-Year Plan of the Stalin era, Pravda published Lenin's article

for the first time on January 20, 1929. The message of the article was met with an enthusiastic response from many Soviet workers.

On August 30, 1935, Alexei Stakhanov a Donbass coalminer set a Soviet record of mining 102 tons of coal in one shift which normally took the average Soviet worker up to fourteen shifts to produce. Stakhanov's record motivated Soviet workers in a broad drive to increase production for the State and it became known as the 'Stakhanov movement'. Millions of workers became involved in the movement to innovate and improve labour production for the State. This became the basis for the socialist competition awards for labour excellence. A worker receiving an award badge labeled 'Udarnik' signified the worker as a 'shock worker' or 'Stakhan-ovite', meaning the worker was a high producer at his or her factory or farm. This programme was used as an incentive for production throughout the USSR.

The State Planning Commission (GOSPLAN) and the Council of Ministers controlled the economy in the Soviet

'Udarnik' Shockworker of Communist Labour Award Pin, c. 1950s. **$35-$45**

Far left: 'Udarnik' Shockworker of Communist Labour Award Pennant, c. 1950s. Silk, 19" x 11". **$30-$45**

Left: Department of Communist Labour Banner, c. 1950s. Silk, 18" x 11". **$30-$45**

Left: 'Udarnik' Shockworker of Communist Labour Award Pin and Award Booklet (unissued), c. 1970s-1980s. **$15-$25**
Slogan on left: We Will Come to the Victory of Communist Labour. V Ulyanov (Lenin)
Text on right: CERTIFICATE 'Udarnik' Shockworker of Communist Labour.

Above and below: 'Udarnik' Shockworker Labour Award Banner, c. 1960s. Silk, 16" x 22". **$35-$45**
Text on front: 'Udarnik' Shockworker of Communist Labour.
Text on back: For Achieving High Marks in a Socialist Competition.

Right: Labour Silk Award Banners.
1. 15 1/2" x 11", c. 1970s. **$25-$35**
2. 24" x 15", c. 1980s. **$35-$55**
Slogan on top: "We Will Come to the Victory of Communist Labour!" V.I. Lenin
Text on bottom: Collective Communist Labour.

Union on the basis of priorities set by the Communist Party of the Soviet Union (CPSU). The State controlled the economy through a guideline known as the 'Plan'. The economic 'Plan' covered time periods ranging from as short as a month to up to the Five-Year Plan and was tailored for each factory.

By the mid-1970s, the Soviet industrial economy actually caught up with the West in areas such as steel production, mining of coal and iron ore, manufacturing of railroad locomotives and cement. But this is not representative when you consider the overall economic production of the Western economies.

Approximately an eighth of the Soviet gross national product went towards military production. The result was an enormous expenditure on weaponry and other military items. In the factories that produced military products there were military generals and officers that supervised the quality control of the military items being manufactured. The substandard items were rejected and were dumped onto the civilian market.

In some factories making a particular item, the assembly lines were divided into three sections, military, export, and domestic civilian. The military assembly line would be composed of the most experienced workers, the newest machinery and the strictest quality control. The export section would get the second best and the domestic civilian last. This is the reason why civilian consumer goods lacked in quality and were often in short supply.

During the Soviet era factory managers often 'fudged' production results to satisfy the 'Plan' when production results were not met. Factory managers were also known to underestimate actual production capacity at their factories and they also made sure the production quotas were not exceeded by more than one or two percent. Otherwise GOSPLAN could

50th Year of the State Planning Commission (GOSPLAN) 1921-1971 Award Badge, c. 1971. **$25-$45**

The Law of Honourary Work Banner, c. 1970s-1980s. **$45-$65**
Silk, 37 1/2" x 24 1/2".
Text on front: By Working for Society, You Work for Yourself.
Labour for the Nation – the Highest Happiness.
It is Not Enough to be a Good Performer of a Given
Assignment – Work Creatively, Truly Communistically.
Knowledge and Experience for the Cause of the Introduction of Modern Techniques – Is Everyone's Concern.
A Minute of Work – Is the Nation's Wealth.
Made with Your Own Hands – It Must Be the Best.
Rejects in Work – Is a Disgrace, Lets Down Co-Workers.
Labourer's Conscience is Stronger than the OTK (Technical Control Department).
Study Constantly, Studying - is the Mother of Skill, With Your Knowledge – Teach Others.
If You are Behind, Ask Your Friend for Help, Better To Ask then Fall Behind, Bring Beauty Into Labour and Life.
At Work, In the Family, Among Friends, Remember: You are the Worker, Do Not Stain Your High Standing.
Where Workers Appear, There is No Place for Hooliganism, Alcoholism, Parasitism.

issue production targets that would be difficult for the factory to meet, as would be dictated in future economic 'Plans'. Workers were also careful not to overproduce and exceed their piecework quotas or their targets would go up as well.

Shortages of parts and raw materials for factory production were often in short supply as the economy was rigidly interlocked. Factories received their supplies from designated suppliers which were dictated by GOSPLAN. If the factory was short of supplies for production, the manager could not simply turn to another supplier for the goods. Often factory managers would collect hidden reserves of raw materials and parts in order to fulfill the 'Plan's' requirements.

In some factories the month's work went forward in three distinct ten-day periods. The workers often called the first ten days the 'hibernation', the second ten-day period the 'hot time', and finally the last ten days the 'storming'. During the 'hibernation' stage, key supplies were missing and many workers would be absent and as a result little production was achieved. During the 'hot time', parts or raw materials started to trickle in from suppliers and production picked up. During the 'storming' the final last ten days of the month, the rest of the supplies arrived and work was done frantically to meet the months production quotas. In many cases a factory would produce eighty percent of the monthly production quotas during the 'storming', the last ten days of the month. If production quotas were not met at the end of the 'storming', managers might falsify their monthly production report to stay out of trouble with the Ministers.

In the socialist economy of the Soviet Union private enterprise was not approved by the State, though there were some exceptions. Workers on the Kolkhozes (collective farms) were allowed to grow produce on their own small gardens and sell limited quantities of it at the local markets. Generally speaking most of the entrepreneurs conducting private business for individual profit was done in the underground economy which was rampant in the USSR. Items that were difficult to find in the State stores were sold by black-market merchants on street corners or in other hidden places and sold to the general public. Another example of the underground economy was the exchange of favours and services by people that were skilled in different trades. In the factories, workers would produce goods for an underground entrepreneur that would in turn pay the workers for the goods and would sell them on the black-market for profit.

In the Soviet communist economy people's incomes were virtually the same for all work done within the system, includ-

Labour Award Banner, c. 1980s. **$250-$350**
Velvet, 66" x 51".
Slogan on front:
Top: Workers of All Countries, Unite!
Bottom: "We Will Come to the Victory of Communist Labour!" V.I. Lenin
Text on back: Enterprise of Communist Labour.

'Udarnik' Shockworker at the Completion of a Five-Year Plan USSR Award Badges. **$15-$20**
1. 9th Five-Year Plan (1971-1975).
2. 10th Five-Year Plan (1976-1980).
3. 12th Five-Year Plan (1986 -1990).

ing government officials, factory administrators, and the workers themselves. Rewards and incentives for good work for the State were provided by the CPSU in the form of decorations such as pins, badges, medals, orders and also award pennants and banners. These were not only issued to individuals but also to factories, collective farms and institutions as a whole. Some of the award banners were awarded at the completion of a Five-Year Plan when a factory or collective farm succeeded in reaching or exceeding the production quotas required by GOSPLAN. Individuals were also rewarded for their efforts as well and these decorations and awards could be given at a monthly or yearly basis and also at the completion of a Five-Year Plan.

The Soviet economy was a centralized economy and by the 1980s, it was unable to keep up with free-enterprise economies of the West. The standard of living for the citizens of the

Soviet Union was lower than that of the citizens in the West. Mikhail Gorbachev in the late 1980s tried to revive the ailing economy through the reforms of 'glasnost' (openness) and 'peristroika' (restructuring). This order of events ultimately resulted in the collapse of the Soviet Empire.

By the mid-1990s, State workers had not received payment of back wages from the government to the order of $8 billion. The unions were demanding their back wages and changes in government policy. The problem was widespread and Mikhail Gorbachev who ushered in this new era, said that sixty percent of the Russian population were living in poverty but believes it could be as high as eighty percent.

Today the citizens of Russia have had to adjust to the capitalist free-enterprise system, which has been applied as a 'shock treatment' to its socialistic system..

Five-Year Plan Silk Award Banners.
1. 68" x 43", c. 1970s. **$115-$155**
2. 64" x 40", c. 1980s. **$95-$135**
Slogans on front -
Top left: Workers of All Countries, Unite!
Bottom: Challenge Banner for Achieving High Marks in a Socialist Competition.
Text on back: Glory Union of Soviet Socialist Republics!

Labour Award Banner, c. 1970s. **$250-$350**
Velvet, 67" x 47".
Slogans on front -
Top left: Workers of All Countries, Unite!
Bottom: Challenge Banner for Achieving High Marks in a Socialist Competition.
Slogan on back: Turn Plans of the Party into Reality!

Glory to 'Perestroika' Labour Banner, c. 1980s. **$35-$45**
Velvet, 18" x 12".
Text on back: Glory to the Foremost Workers of Labour the Innovators of Restructuring.

Order of Red Banner Labour.
Awarded for outstanding labour contributions in production, science, culture, education, health care, etc. Instituted September 7, 1928 and over 1,200,000 were issued.
1. screwback version, c. 1936-1943. **$450-$475**
2. large body version on ribbon suspension, c. 1943-early 1950s. **$45-$85**
3. medium body version on ribbon suspension, c. 1950s. **$45-$85**
4. small body version with early style hammer and sickle on ribbon suspension, c. 1960s. **$35-$65**
5. small body version with late style hammer and sickle on ribbon suspension, c. 1970s-1980s. **$35-$65**
Slogan on front: Workers of All Countries, Unite!

Order of the Badge of Honour.
Awarded for labour achievements, scientific research, social activities to improve all areas of national life. Instituted November 25, 1935 and over 1,500,000 were issued.
1. screwback version, c. 1936-1943. **$200-$250**
2. flatback version on ribbon suspension, c. 1943-1950s. **$45-$85**
3. concave back version on ribbon suspension, c. 1950s-1988. **$35-$65**
Slogan on front: Workers of All Countries, Unite!

Left: People's Commissariat of Construction **$85-$95**
Excellence in a Socialist Competition Award Badge.

Right: People's Commissariat of Electrical Power **$85-$95**
Excellence in a Socialist Competition Award Badge.

BELOW: During the 1930s until 1946, the People's Commissariats (Narkomat) were the government agencies that controlled industry. The following are some of the labour award badges issued during this time period.

Left: People's Commissariat of the Coal Industry **$85-$95**
Excellence in a Socialist Competition Award Badge.

Right: People's Commissariat of Ferrous Metals **$85-$95**
Excellence in a Socialist Competition Award Badge.

Left: People's Commissariat of Electrical Power **$85-$95**
Excellence in a Socialist Competition Award Badge.

Right: People's Commissariat of Machine Building **$85-$95**
Excellence in a Socialist Competition Award Badge.

People's Commissariat of Heavy Machine Building **$85-$95**
Excellence in a Socialist Competition Award Badge.

THIS PAGE: In 1946, the Council of People's Commissars (Sovnarkom) was changed to the Council of Ministers. The People's Commissariats (Narkomat) were then changed to become Ministries which were the government agencies that controlled industry. The following are some of the labour award badges issued after 1946.

Left: Ministry of the Coal Industry **$85-$95**
Excellence in a Socialist Competition Award Badge, c. 1950s.

Right: Ministry of the Electrical Power Industry **$85-$95**
Excellence in a Socialist Competition award Badge, c. 1950s.

Ministry of the Coal Industry **$85-$95**
Excellence in a Socialist Competition Award Badges.
1. Stalin/Lenin version, c. before 1953.
2. Lenin version, c. after 1953.

Left: Ministry of the Electrical Power Industry **$85-$95**
Excellence in a Socialist Competition Award Badge, c. 1960s.

Right: Ministry of the Electrical Power Industry **$85-$95**
Excellence in a Socialist Competition Award Badge, c. 1970s-1980s.

Left: Ministry of the Oil Industry **$85-$95**
Excellence in a Socialist Competition Award Badge, c. 1950s.

Right: Ministry of the Oil Industry, Eastern Regions **$85-$95**
Excellence in a Socialist Competition Award Badge, c. 1950s.

Left: Ferrous Metallurgy Industry **$85-$95**
Excellence in a Socialist Competition, c. 1950s.

Right: Ministry of the Non-Ferrous Metallurgy Industry **$85-$95**
Excellence in a Socialist Competition Award Badge, c. 1950s.

Left: Ministry of the Construction Industry Excellence in a Socialist Competition Award Badges.
1. c. 1950s-1960s. **$85-$95**
2. c. 1970s. **$15-$25**

Right: Ministry of the Transport Machinery Industry **$85-$95**
Excellence Award Badge, c. 1950s.

Honoured Railway Employee Award Badges.
1. miniature version in sterling silver, c. 1930s. **$185-$215**
2. sterling silver version, c. 1930s-1950s. **$85-$115**
3. bronze version, c. 1930s-1950s. **$65-$85**
4. brass, c. 1970s-1980s. **$65-$85**

Excellence in a Socialist Competition of Railway Transport Award Badges.
1. German silver, c. 1950s-1960s. **$65-$75**
2. Aluminum, c. 1970s-1980s. **$25-$35**

'Udarnik' Shockworker of 'Stalin's Calling' Railway Labour Campaign.
1. 3-piece, c. 1930s. **$65-$85**
2. 1-piece, c. 1940s-1950s. **$35-$45**

Left: Excellent Engine Operator Award Badge, c. 1940s-1950s. **$45-$65**

Right: Honoured Polar Travel Award Badge, c. 1960s. **$55-$65**

Honoured Worker of the Merchant Fleet Award Badges.
1. c. 1940s. **$95-$115**
2. c. 1950s. **$55-$65**
3. c. 1960s. **$55-$65**

PAGES 107-108: The Soviet Government declared nationwide Socialist Competitions between factories, collectives, groups of workers ('Brigade'), departments, and between the workers themselves, as a means of an incentive to promote production. Factories and collectives would be awarded with large banners for their achievements, while individuals would receive award pennants and badges for their accomplishments. The Soviet people would wear their decorations with pride. The following are some of the award badges and banners.

Below: Winner in a Socialist Competition Award Pennants.
1. Silk, c. 1970s-1980s, 18" x 10 1/2". **$20-$35**
2. Silk, c. 1970s-1980s, 24" x 16". **$20-$35**
3. Velvet, c. 1970s, 23" x 15". **$45-$55**

Below, far right: Best Brigade Award Banner, c. 1970s-1980s. **$20-$35**
Silk, 18" x 10 1/2".
Text: Best Brigade (group of shockworkers).

Winner in a Socialist Competition Award Badges.
1. 1973, 1974 (Style of the ninth Five-Year Plan badges). **$10-$15**
2. 1977 (Style of the tenth Five-Year Plan badges). **$10-$15**

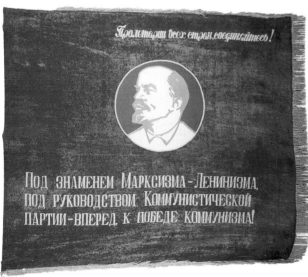

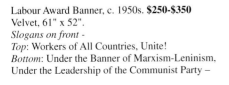

Labour Award Banner, c. 1950s. **$250-$350**
Velvet, 61" x 52".
Slogans on front -
Top: Workers of All Countries, Unite!
Bottom: Under the Banner of Marxism-Leninism,
Under the Leadership of the Communist Party –

Forward, to the Victory of Communism!
Text on back -
Top: To the Complex of the Building Brigade (group of shockworkers).
Winner in a Socialist Competition.
Bottom: From the City of Rostovskii Regional Executive Committee Regional
Council of Trade Unions Regional Committee of the CPSU.

Labour Award Banner, c. 1970s. **$250-$350**
Velvet, 66" x 51".
Slogans on front -
Top: Workers of All Countries, Unite!
Bottom: Under the Banner of Marxism-Leninism,
Under the Leadership of the Communist Party – Forward, to the Victory of Communism!
Text on back -
Top: Council of Ministers Union SSR and
All-Union Central Committee of the Trade Unions
Bottom: Winner in an All-Union Socialist Competition.

Labour Award Banner, c. 1980s. **$300-$400**
Velvet, 66"x 51".
Slogans on front -
Top: Workers of All Countries, Unite!
Bottom: Under the Leadership of the CPSU – Forward, to the Victory of Communism!
Text on back -
Top: TsK (Central Committee) of the CPSU,
Council of Ministers USSR,
VTsSPS (All-Union Central Council of Trade Unions) and TsK (Central Committee) of the VLKSM (All-Union Leninist Communist Union of Youth).
Bottom: Winner in an All-Union Socialist Competition.

Left: Labour Award Banner, c. 1970s-1980s. **$20-$35**
Silk, 24" x 13".
Text on front -
Top: Glory to Lenin's Party!
Middle: Best Leader
Bottom: For Achieving High Marks in a Socialist Competition.
Slogan on back: We Will Come to the Victory of Communist Labour V.I. Lenin

Left: For Active Work in the Trade Unions Award Badge, c. 1970s. **$35-$55**

Right: Excellent State Labour Reserves Award Badge, c. 1950s. **$55-$65**

All-Union Central Council of Trade Unions Award Badge, c. 1970s. **$55-$65**
Text on back: For Strengthening the Cooperation of the Arts and Labour.

Trade Union of Metallurgy Badge, c. 1970s-1980s. **$25-$45**

Labour Award Banners, c. 1970s-1980s. **$20-$35**
Silk, 20" x 14 1/2".
1. The Best Production Department.
2. The Best Worker of Mechanization.

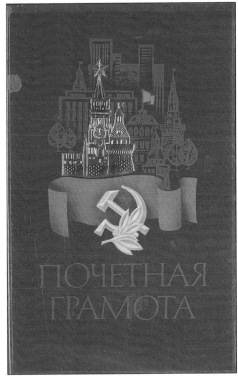

Honourary Award Document for Labour (unissued), c. 1985. **$10-$15**
Text on left: The First Productive Strength in all Humanity is the Worker, Labourer. V.I. Lenin

Excellence GOSSNAB (State Committee for Technical-Material Supply) USSR Award Badge, c. 1970s-1980s. **$30-$45**
This Committee procured and distributed supplies to the factories to complete the manufacturing of products as dictated by GOSPLAN (The State Planning Commission).

Honourary Award Document for Labour (unissued), c. 1983. **$10-$15**
Text on front left: There is No Higher Title in the World than a Working Person
Text on right: Initiation of a Worker
Text on back: Dear Friend …

Today in your life is a big occasion – you became a worker, joining our working collective. From now on you are a heir and successor of the glorious revolutionary, fighting and labouring traditions of the working class.

Courageously and happily attain an independent life. Be always loyal to our socialist Homeland, Communist party. Piously obey soviet laws and traditions. Above all respect industrialness and mastering, honesty and truthfulness, collectiveness and friendship, irreconcilable with deficiency, moral purity – all that, from which is formed a communistic relationship to labour.

The country needs your labour. Be an active participant in socialistic competition. It will make your life more interesting, richer spiritually, will help to obtain the secrets of mastering faster.

Love your profession. Don't be afraid of difficulty, go only forward. Know: There is no more truthful way to happiness than the way of labour. Grasp the experience of the elders, take example from the leaders, from those, who are called masters of the business. Work such, that, those who look at you and what you produce with your hands, could say: This is a real worker!

Let our congratulations remind you about this happy day of the initiation of a worker, about the oath – carry with honour through your whole life a high name as a builder of communism. Heartily greet you in this significant day and wish you health, success, happiness!

Enterprise manager
Secretary of the Party Organization
Trade Union Organization leader
Secretary of the Komsomol Organization.

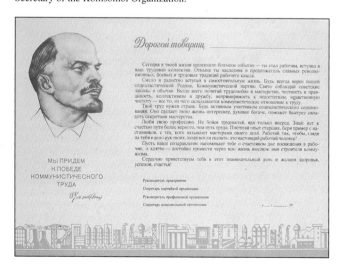

Order of Labour Glory.
Awarded to workers in industry, construction, transportation, agriculture, and to educators. Can be awarded in 1st, 2nd and 3rd classes. Instituted January 18, 1974 and over 700,000 were issued.
1. 3rd class initial version with separate hammer and sickle riveted to body, c. 1974-1976. **$45-$85**
2. 3rd class one-piece construction, c. 1976-1991. **$35-$65**

  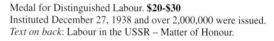 

Medal for Valiant Labour. **$20-$30**
Instituted December 27, 1938 and over 2,000,000 were issued.
Text on back: Labour in the USSR – Matter of Honour.

Medal for Distinguished Labour. **$20-$30**
Instituted December 27, 1938 and over 2,000,000 were issued.
Text on back: Labour in the USSR – Matter of Honour.

Foremost Worker in an International Socialist Competition Award Badge, c. 1970s. **$55-$65**

Right: Medal for Veteran of Labour. **$20-$30**
Instituted January 18, 1974 and over 3,500,000 were issued.
1. initial version.
2. final version.
Text on back: For Longstanding and Conscientious Labour.

Veteran of Labour Award Badge, c. 1970s-1980s. **$15-$20**

Medal for the 100th Anniversary of Lenin's Birth. **$20-$30**
Awarded for valiant labour. Instituted November 5, 1969 and approximately 10,000,000 were issued.
Text on back: For Valiant Labour On the Commemoration of the 100th Year Anniversary of the Birth of V.I. Lenin.

Excellence in a Socialist Competition During the 100th Anniversary of Lenin's Birth 1870-1970 Award Pin, c. 1970. **$10-$15**

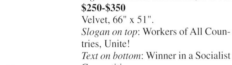

Right: Labour Award Banner, c. 1970. **$250-$350**
Velvet, 66" x 51".
Slogan on top: Workers of All Countries, Unite!
Text on bottom: Winner in a Socialist Competition
In Honour of the 100 Year of Birth of V.I. Lenin.

Above: Excellence in a Socialist Competition in the RSFSR Award Badge, c. 1950s-1960s. **$25-$35**

Above right: Excellence in Local Industry of the RSFSR Award Badge, c. 1960s. **$25-$35**

Right: Excellence in a Socialist Competition on an Agricultural Farm in the RSFSR Award Badge, c. 1970s. **$20-$30**

Central Council of the All-Union Association of Invention and Rationalization (VOIR) Banner, c. 1986. **$15-$25**
Silk, 16" x 11 1/2".
Text on front: The Best Creative Workers Association 1986
Text on back: Central Council VOIR.

Labour Award Banner, c. 1970s-1980s. **$20-$35**
Silk, 24" x 14 1/2".
Slogans on front -
Slogan in ribbon: Labour in the USSR – Matter of Honour, Glory, Valour and Heroism!
Middle: Turn Plans of the Party into Reality!
Slogan on back in ribbon: We Will Come to the Victory of Communist Labour!

Labour Award Banner, c. 1970s-1980s. **$20-$35**
Silk, 26" x 14".
Slogan on front: We Will Come to the Victory of Communist Labour!
V Ulyanov (Lenin)
Text on back -
Top: Long Live the Great Soviet People – Building Communism!
Bottom: For Achieving High Marks in a Socialist Competition.

Labour Award Banner, c. 1970s-1980s. **$20-$35**
Silk, 22" x 13".
Slogan on front: "We Will Come to the Victory of Communist Labour!"
V Ulyanov (Lenin)

Labour Award Pennant, c. 1970s-1980s. **$15-$25**
Silk, 18" x 10 1/2".
A blank pennant could be used to attach award pins and badges.

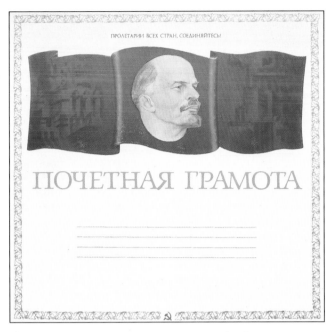

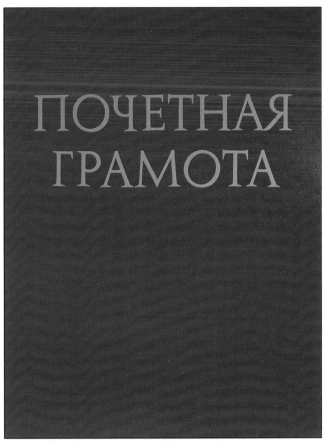

Honourary Award Document for Labour (unissued). **$10-$15**
1. "Plakat" Publishers Moscow by A. Smislov, c. 1982.
2. "Plakat" Publishers Moscow by B. Verizhnikov, c. 1988.
Text: Workers of All Countries, Unite!
HONOURARY AWARD DOCUMENT
For Achieving the Highest Results in a Socialist Competition
Rewards …

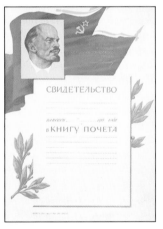

Left: Certificate for being inscribed in the Book of Honour (unissued), c. 1967.
$10-$15
Text on top: We Will Come to the Victory of Communist Labour! V Ulyanov
(Lenin)

Right: Award Document for Labour (unissued), c. 1976.

All-Union Exhibition of Economic Achievements (VDNKh) Awards, c. 1970s-1980s.
1. VDNKh - USSR Membership Pin. **$5-$10**
2. VDNKh - Youth Participation, Gold Medal. **$20-$30**
3. VDNKh - Gold Medal Winner. **$20-$30**
4. For Success in the Nation's Economy USSR, Gold Medal. **$20-$25**
5. For Success in the Nation's Economy USSR, Silver Medal. **$20-$25**
These awards were given to Soviet workers, farmers, scientists and inventors for special achievements in the nation's economy. The Exhibition of Economic Achievements was created as a show place of the finest achievements of the Soviet State. It was first opened in 1939 during the Stalin era. At the entrance to the exhibition, the famous statue of the 'Worker and Collective Farmer' is seen on the obverse of the medals.

All-Union Agricultural Exhibition (VSKhV).
1. VSKhV Membership Pin, c. 1930s-1950s. **$20-$25**
2. VSKhV Gold Medal for Participation, c. 1970s-1980s. **$20-$25**

Photograph of the 'Worker and Collective Farmer' Monument by V. Mukhina.

1947 – 30th Year of the October Revolution Land of Socialism Commemorative Badge, c. 1947. **$35-$55**

State Commission for the Electrification of Russia (GOELRO).
1. 50th Year GOELRO Plan Commemorative Pin, c. 1970. **$5-$10**
2. GOELRO Pin, c. 1970s. **$5-$10**
In December 1920 at the 8th Congress of Soviets, Lenin proclaimed that the "Electrification of Russia" was the key to the success of communism.

Oil on Canvas Painting of Lenin proclaiming the "Electrification of Russia" (GOELRO) at the 8th Congress of Soviets, December 1920. c. 1950s-1960s, 96" x 60". **$5500-$7500**

1 May – May Day Commemorative Badge, c. 1940s. **$35-$45**

Above right: Glory to Labour Pin, c. 1970s-1980s. **$5-$10**

Right: Knowledge for the Nation Pin, c. 1970s. **$5-$10**

Above and right: Lenin's Communist 'Subbotnik' Pin and Arm Patch. **$25-$35**

Text on pin: Lenin's Communist Subbotnik.
Text on arm patch: Participant in a Communist Subbotnik.
Once a year on a Saturday near Labour Day (May 1), the Soviet people volunteered one day of free work for the State.

SIX

COMMUNIST YOUTH ORGANIZATIONS

The Octoberists

The Octoberists was the first organization a Soviet citizen became a member of during his or her first formal years in school. The Octoberists organization was founded in 1923-24 and catered to children between the ages of seven and nine. The Octoberists wore a pin in the shape of a red star with the head of the 'baby Lenin' in its center. The organization prepared the young children for their next move into the Young Pioneers at the age of ten.

Octoberists Membership Pins.
1. c. 1960s-1970s. **$5-$10**
2. c. 1970s-1980s. **$5-$10**

The Young Pioneers

The next organization for Soviet youth was the Young Pioneers and catered to young people between the ages of ten to fourteen. The Young Pioneer organization was founded in 1922 and was an auxiliary to the Komsomol. The Young Pioneers Central Council was under the overall direction of the Komsomol. All school children of the appropriate age were eligible to join their local Young Pioneer Organization. If accepted they had to take the Young Pioneer oath, respect the pioneer laws, and wear the red Young Pioneer scarf. The scarf had three corners representing the unity of the Young Pioneers, Komsomol, and Communists. The Young Pioneers also wore a pin, which had the bust of Lenin on it with a flame above his head and the slogan "Always Ready!" written across it. The organization taught their members to fight for the cause of the Communist Party, to be persistent in studies and labour, and assist the younger generation in the spirit of communism and morality.'

Left: 'Baby Lenin' Pin, c. 1950s. **$15-$20**
Right: 1924-1944 'Baby Lenin' Commemorative Pin. **$15-$20**

The classic Young Pioneer hero that became a symbol for the Young Pioneers was Pavlik Morozov. During the forced collectivization of the 'Kulaks' (better-off peasants) during the Stalin era of the 1930s, young children learned that Stalin wanted them to be vigilant. It was the youngster's duty to report 'counterrevolutionary' activity to the Soviet authorities even if their parents were involved. Parents were sent to jail for careless words spoken about the regime in front of their own children. It was in 1932, that Pavlik Morozov at the age of twelve reported to the authorities that his father stole a sack of grain from the State farm. His father subsequently was taken away by the authorities and shot. A few days later the villagers in the area killed Pavlik in revenge, only to be arrested and executed themselves. Pavlik Morozov became a hero for doing his duty for the State. The Palace of Culture of the Young Pioneers in Moscow was named in his honour and a statue of him was put up in his village. Pavlik was immortalized by the Communist Party. Pavlik Morozov was less vigorously celebrated as the years after Stalin's death went on but the code of the Young Pioneers still promotes not only civic duty but political consciousness among the Soviet youth, 'A pioneer is loyal to the homeland, Party, communism.'

Young Pioneer Membership Pins, c. 1970s-1980s. **$5-$10**
Slogan in crest: Always Ready!

Young Pioneer Leader's Pin,
c. 1970s-1980s. **$5-$10**
Slogan in crest: Always Ready!

Young Pioneer Flag, c. 1980s. **$35-$55**
Silk, 23" x 18".
Slogan in crest: Always Ready!

Young Pioneer Pennant, c. 1980s.
$25-$35
Silk, 17" x 11".
Slogan in crest: Always Ready!
Slogan beneath crest: Be Ready!

Young Pioneer 'For Active Work' Pin, c. 1970s-1980s. **$5-$10**

Young Pioneer Marching Flags.
Silk, 38" x 30".
1. c. 1970s. **$65-$85**
2. c. 1980s. **$65-$85**
Slogan at top: To Fight for the Cause of the Communist Party of the Soviet Union.
Slogan in middle: Be Ready!
Slogan in crest: Always ready!

Left: 40th Year of the Young Pioneer Organization Pin, c. 1962. **$35-$45**

Right: 50th Year of the Young Pioneers Commemorative Pin, c. 1972. **$5-$10**
Text: 50th Year of the All-Union Pioneer Organization
In the Name of V.I. Lenin.

50th Year of the Young Pioneers Commemorative Table Medallion, c. 1972.
$30-$45
Text: 50th Year 1922 1972 of the All-Union Pioneer Organization In the Name of V.I. Lenin

Above: Young Pioneer Banner, c. 1970s. **$25-$35**
Slogan in crest: Always Ready!
Text beneath crest: Right Flank of the Pioneer Troops.

Right: Young Pioneer Flag Pole Top Ribbon, c. 1982. **$15-$20**
Silk, 23" x 4".
Text: Commemorative Jubilee Ribbon for the Right Flank Troops in Honour of the 60th Year of the All-Union Pioneer Organization
In the Name of V.I. Lenin.

Young Pioneer 1st class Pin, c. 1950s.
$20-$30

Young Pioneer Musical Instrument Parade Banner, c. 1970-1980s. **$20-$35**
Silk, 13" x 11".
Slogan at top: To Fight for the Cause of the Communist Party of the Soviet Union
Slogan in crest: Always Ready!
Slogan beneath crest: Be Ready!

Solemn Promise of the Pioneers of the Soviet Union Banner, c. 1970s.
$65-$85
Silk, 40" x 33".
Pioneer Oath: see Pioneer Oath Banner on the next page.

Right: Laws of the Pioneers of the Soviet Union Banner, c. 1985.
Silk, 29" x 16". **$45-$55**
Slogan at top: To Fight for the Cause of the Communist Party of the Soviet Union Be Ready!
Slogan in crest: Always Ready!
Pioneer Motto: Pioneer loyal to the homeland, Party, communism. Pioneer is ready to become the member of the Komsomol.
Pioneer keeps up with the heroes of the struggle and of labour.
Pioneer respectfully remembers the fallen fighters and is ready to become a defender of the homeland.
Pioneer is persistent in studies, labour and sport.
Pioneer - is an honest and loyal friend, always brave to stand for the truth.
Pioneer - is a comrade and leader of the Octoberists.
Pioneer - is a friend to Pioneers and children of the working class of all the countries.

Far right: Pioneer Oath Banner, c. 1970s-1980s. **$65-$85**
Silk, 42" x 26".
Slogan at top: To Fight for the Cause of the Communist Party of the Soviet Union Be Ready!
Slogan in crest: Always Ready! Title: Solemn Promise of the Pioneers of the Soviet Union
Pioneer Oath: I (Family, Name), Entering the Ranks of the All-Union Pioneer Organization In the Name of Vladimir Ilyich Lenin, In Front of My Friends Solemnly Promise: To Dearly Love My Homeland, Live, Study and Fight by the Will of the Great Lenin, the Way of the Communist Party, and Always Obey the Laws of the Pioneers of the Soviet Union.

Komsomol (VLKSM)

Komsomol (All-Union Leninist Communist Union of Youth) was the last and most important youth organization a young person could join in the Soviet Union. It catered to young people between the ages of eighteen and twenty-eight and served as an important training ground for Party and other Soviet officials. In order to become a member of the Komsomol the individual had to be recommended by a member of the Communist Party or by two members of the Komsomol itself. The Komsomol was founded on October 29, 1918. It was an auxiliary of the Communist Party and throughout its history was closely controlled by the Party and subordinate to its pur-

poses. The Komsomol organization won many orders for its efforts to help build the Soviet nation. In 1928 it won the Order of the Red Banner for its participation during the Civil War; in 1931 it won the Order of Red Banner Labour for its achievements during the first Five-Year Plan; in 1945 it won the Order of Lenin for its participation during the 'Great Patriotic War'; in 1948 it won the Order of Lenin for socialist construction on its thirtieth anniversary; in 1956 it won the Order of Lenin for participating in the 'virgin lands' agricultural project; and in 1968 it won the Order of the October Revolution for its achievements in science on its fiftieth anniversary.

About half of the Soviet population within the appropriate age group were members of the Komsomol. The Komsomol

Komsomol Membership Badges.
1. c. 1940s. **$20-$30**
2. c. 1970s-1980s (civilian pin back). **$5-$10**
3. c. 1970s-1980s (military screwback). **$10-$15**

was structured in essentially the same format as the Communist Party of the Soviet Union (CPSU). The Komsomol had a Congress, which met every five years and elected a Central Committee that met every six months. The Komsomol also had a Secretariat to administer the work of the organization. The political process of the Komsomol was similar to that of the CPSU as members of the Congress and the Central Committee were chosen and accepted by the leaders of the Komsomol organization.

Komsomol members received preferential treatment for admission to the CPSU. In the 1970s and 1980s, more than seventy percent of the Party recruits were from the Komsomol. Komsomol membership and service was also taken into account for employment opportunities and for higher education admission. It also increased the possibility for an individual to receive honours, titles and awards. Members of the Komsomol organization participated in politics, industry, agriculture, and in the military, building socialism in the USSR.

The day of the Birth of the Komsomol Commemorative Pin, 29 October 1918, c. 1970s. **$5-$10**

Komsomol Orders Pin Set, c. 1960s-1970s. **$10-$15 each**
1. 1945 - Order of Lenin for Participation During the 'Great Patriotic War' (World War II).
2. 1948 - Order of Lenin on the 30th Year of the Komsomol for Socialist Construction.
3. 1956 - Order of Lenin for Participating in the 'Virgin Lands' Agricultural Project.
4. 1968 - Order of the October Revolution on the 50th Year of the Komsomol for Achievements in Science.

50th Year of the Komsomol (VLKSM) Set of Award Medallions with Case, c. 1968. **$145-$165**
1. 1918-1968 Only by Working Together with the Workers and Peasants is it Possible to Become a Real Communist. V. Ulyanov (Lenin)
2. TsKI (Central Executive Committee) USSR To Commemorate the VLKSM's Merit of Battle at the Fronts of the Civil War in the Period of 1919-1920 ... Rewards it the Order of the Red Banner, 23 February 1928.
3. For the Initiative Shown in the Matter of Outstanding Performance and in a Socialist Competition, Guaranteeing a Successful Completion of the Five-Year Plan ... Rewards the VLKSM Order of Red Banner Labour, 21 January 1931.
4. For Outstanding Merits for the Homeland in the Years of the Patriotic War USSR Against Hitler's Germany ... Rewards the VLKSM Order of Lenin, 14 June 1945.
5. For Outstanding Merits for the Homeland... and Active Participation in Socialist Construction, In Association with the 30th Year of the VLKSM... Rewards the Order of Lenin, 29 October 1948.
6. To Mark the Selfless and Fruitful Labour of Members of the Komsomol Soviet Youth in Successful Development of the Virgin Lands, Rewards the VLKSM Order of Lenin.

Komsomol Congress Delegates Badges. **$65-$85**
1. XV
2. XVI
3. XVIII
4. XIX
5. XX

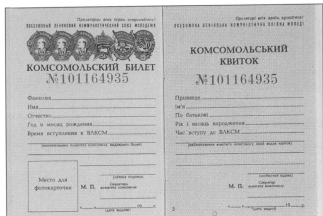

Right: Komsomol I.D. Booklet (unissued), c. 1970s-1980s. **$10-$15**

Left: XXX Years of the Komsomol Commemorative Badge, c. 1948. **$45-$55**

Right: 40th Year of the Komsomol Commemorative Badge, c. 1958. **$45-$55**

Above: 50th Year of the Komsomol Commemorative Pins, c. 1968. **$5-$10**

Right: 50th Year of the Komsomol Pin and Arm Patch, c. 1968. **$15-$20**

Komsomol Bronze Lenin Table Medallion, c. 1970. **$80-$95**
Text on back: The Name and the Cause of Lenin Will Live Forever! 1870-1970 TsK VLKSM (Central Committee of the Komsomol).

70th Year of the Komsomol Commemorative Pin, c. 1988. **$5-$10**

XVIII Komsomol Congress Commemorative Pin. **$5-$10**

XIX Komsomol Congress Commemorative Badge. **$55-$65**

XX Komsomol Congress Pin Set. **$5-$10**

Komsomol Valiant Labour Award Badge, c. 1980s. **$45-$55**
Text on back: Badge from the TsK (Central Committee) VLKSM (Komsomol) for Valiant Labour.

Master of the Golden Hands Komsomol Award Badge, c. 1970s. **$45-$55** Instituted during the 10th Five-Year Plan (1976-1980).

Winner of Youth Technical and Scientific Creativity Prize Komsomol Award Badge, c. 1970s. **$25-$45** Instituted during the 10th Five-Year Plan (1976-1980).

Komsomol Instructor of Youth Award Badge, c. 1970s. **$45-$55**
Text on front: Instructor of Youth.
Text on back: Badge from the VTsSPS (All-Union Central Council of Trade Unions) and TsK VLKSM (Central Committee of the Komsomol).

Left: For Active Work in the Komsomol Pin, c. 1950s-1960s. **$35-$45**
Right: Komsomol In Lenin's Trust Pin, c. 1970s-1980s. **$5-$10**

Right: Komsomol Lenin's Credit Pin, c. 1970s-1980s. **$5-$10**
Awarded for the successful completion of an examination.
Far right: Komsomol 'Udarnik' Shockworker 1974 Award Pin. **$5-$10**

Left: Komsomol 'Udarnik' Shockworker during a Summer Quarter Award Pin, c. 1970s-1980s. **$5-$10**

Right: Komsomol 8th Grade "Study Study Study" Pin, ca 1970s. **$5-$10**

Left: Award Badge from the Central Committee of the Komsomol for an Exemplary Worker of New Construction Projects during the VI Five-Year Plan (1956-1960). **$35-$45**

Right: Award Badge from the Central Committee of the Komsomol for Cultivating the 'Virgin Lands', c. 1950s-1960s. **$35-$45**

Komsomol Award Banner. **$25-$35**
Silk, 16" x 12".
Text on front: 60 Years of the Formation of USSR-Komsomol Shockworkers!
Text on back -
Top: Winner in a Republic Inspection of Work Among the Komsomol Organizations.
Bottom: 'Udmurtskii' Regional Committee of the VLKSM.

Komsomol Organization of Schools Flag, c. 1970s-1980s.
Silk, 38" x 30". **$65-$85**
Slogans on front -
Slogan on top: Workers of All Countries, Unite!
Text on bottom: Komsomol Organization of Schools.
Text on back: All-Union Leninist Communist Union of Youth.

Left: Award Badge from the Central Committee of the Komsomol for a High Harvest of Corn, c. 1960s. **$35-$45**

Right: 50th Anniversary of the Komsomol Organization Award Pin for Work at the Gorkovo Mine No. 8, c. 1968. **$10-$15**

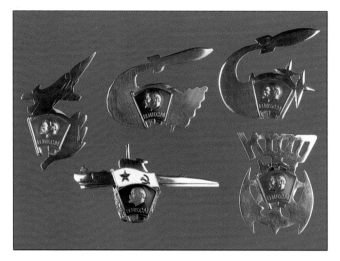

Komsomol Military Participation Badges, c. 1970s-1980s. **$35-$45 each**
1. Soviet Air Force.
2. Air Defence Forces.
3. Strategic Rocket Forces.
4. Soviet Navy Submarine Service.
5. Soviet Navy Pacific Fleet Service.

Left: 50th Year of the Department of Komsomol Workers for the Main Political Administration of the Soviet Army and Navy Pin. **$15-$25**

Right: Komsomol Military Valour Award Badge, c. 1960s-1980s. **$55-$85**

Komsomol Soviet Security Forces Participation Badges (MVD/KGB), c. 1970s-1980s. **$35-$45**

SEVEN

SOVIET MILITARY FORCES

The first legislative act written by Lenin proclaiming the organization of the Red Army was a Declaration of the Rights of the Working and Exploited People. In it he stated, "To ensure the sovereign power of the working people, and to eliminate all possibility of the restoration of the power of the exploiters, the arming of the working people, the creation of a socialist Red Army of workers and peasants and the complete disarming of the propertied classes are hereby decreed."

On January 28, 1918, the Council of People's Commissars (Sovnarkom) and Lenin as its leader signed a decree on the Workers' and Peasant's Red Army.

On February 18, 1918 during World War I, the German army made an offensive against Soviet Russia in the direction of Petrograd the cradle of the Great October Socialist Revolution in an effort to overthrow the Soviet government. On February 21, 1918, the Council of People's Commissars (Sovnarkom) addressed the nation with an appeal calling on the workers and peasants to defend the Soviet Republic. On February 22 and 23, 1918, mass rallies were held in Petrograd, Moscow and in many other cities. The Petrograd Soviet declared February 23, 1918, the 'Day of the Defence of the Socialist Fatherland' and was the day of the mass enlistment of volunteers for the Red Army. This is the reason why 'Soviet Army Day' was celebrated on February 23 in the USSR.

On March 13, 1918, Trotsky the first Commissar of War was made Chairman of the Supreme War Council which had been set-up in Petrograd to create the Red Army.

Recruitment for the Red Army was originally intended to be voluntary. Lenin envisioned a Red Army made up of individuals who were 'revolutionary sympathizers', not 'reactionary'. But by April 1918, the Bolshevik Government issued a

'Serve the Homeland!' Soviet Military Forces Poster. **$25-$35**
"Panorama" Publishers Moscow, c. 1990.

decree making mandatory conscription necessary to increase the size of the Red Army during the Civil War. In the autumn of 1917, the Red Guards had a total number of 100,000 volunteers. The Red Guards were fused into the Red Army and within three years there was a total of 5,000,000 servicemen enlisted.

Jubillee Medals for the Anniversaries of the Soviet Armed Forces.
1. 20th Anniversary, 1918-1938. **$165-$195**
Instituted January 24, 1938 and over 37,000 were issued.
2. 30th Anniversary, 1918-1948. **$35-$55**
Instituted February 22, 1948 and over 3,700,000 were issued.
Text on back: For the Commemoration of the Thirtieth Anniversary of the Soviet Army and Navy 1918-1948.
3. 40th Anniversary, 1918-1958. **$25-$35**
Instituted December 18, 1957 and over 820,000 were issued.
Text on back: For the Commemoration of the Fortieth Anniversary of the Armed Forces of the USSR 1918-1958.
4. 50th Anniversary, 1918-1968. Instituted December 26, 1967 and over 9,500,000 were issued. **$20-$30**
Text on back: Fifty Years of the Armed Forces of the USSR.
5. 60th Anniversary, 1918-1978. Instituted January 28, 1978 and over 10,700,000 were issued. **$20-$30**
Text on back: Sixty Years of the Armed Forces of the USSR.
6. 70th Anniversary, 1918-1988. Instituted January 28, 1988 and over 9,300,000 were issued. **$20-$30**
Text on back: 70 Years of the Armed Forces of the USSR.

Due to the complexity and size of the Civil War, the Bolsheviks recruited ex-czarist officers despite their 'bourgeois' background into the Red Army. They were called 'military specialists' and worked directly under the supervision of the Bolshevik military Commissars.

The Civil War ended in a Bolshevik victory in December 1920. As a result of the calamity of the long Civil War and the economic policy called 'War Communism' which was required to maintain the war effort, the young Soviet economy was in ruins. After the Civil War the Red Army was utilized in the reconstruction of the Russian economy. During the first Five-Year Plan (1928-1932), Soviet industry grew tremendously and along with it the Soviet military grew as well. During the first Five-Year Plan the number of aircraft grew from approximately 1,400 to over 6,600 units and the number of tanks grew from almost 100 to more than 10,000 units.

The years 1937 to 1938 were the years of Stalin's 'purges' of the Soviet Red Army. From May 1937 to September 1938 the victims of the 'purges' in the military included nearly half of the regimental commanders, nearly all brigade commanders, and all commanders of army corps and military districts, as well as members of military councils and heads of political directorates in the military districts, the majority of political commissars in army corps, divisions, and brigades, almost one-third of the regimental commissars, and many instructors at military academies. The most famous victim of the 'purges' was Marshal Tukhachevsky. In all approximately 35,000 officers of all ranks were shot or imprisoned. This immense purge of the military leadership caused serious problems for the Soviet Red Army during the initial stages of the 'Great Patriotic War'.

Stalin was convinced Hitler would not attack the Soviet Union even though Soviet intelligence indicated it was imminent. He was hoping to stay out of the war for several years giving him time to reform and complete his expansion of the Soviet Military Forces. On June 22, 1941, the German Army invaded the USSR. The losses for the Soviet Union in the initial stages of the war were appalling as the Germans captured whole armies and corps. Within several weeks the Germans advanced 500 miles into Soviet territory.

Soviet industry played a major role in mass producing the necessary military hardware to fight the war. The Soviets were fortunate to fight the war on one front which enabled them to concentrate all their resources in one area. The Soviets out produced and overwhelmed the Germans and by the summer of 1944, drove the Nazis back across Central Europe to the borders of Germany itself. In 1945, the Soviet Red Army invaded Germany and captured Berlin. The Soviet Union defeated the Germans and proclaimed victory in World War II. The Soviet Red Army defeated the Germans but the losses for the USSR were staggering as the destruction of towns and villages was horrific and the USSR lost in excess of 20,000,000 people.

50th Year Glory to the Soviet Army 1918-1968 Commemorative Pin Set, c. 1968. **$5-$10**

60th Year of the Order of the Red Banner Soviet Red Army (SKVO) 1918-1978 Commemorative Pin, c. 1978. **$5-$10**

Right: 70th Year of the Armed Forces of the USSR Commemorative Badge, c. 1988. **$35-$45**

9th May - Day of Victory over the Germans in the 'Great Patriotic War' Commemorative Pins, c. 1970s-1980s. **$10-$15**

Right top: Order of the Patriotic War.
Awarded to personnel of the Soviet Armed Forces and NKVD Troops for acts of courage during the 'Great Patriotic War'. Instituted May 20, 1942.
1. 1st class World War II solid gold, screwback version, 1943-1945. Over 325,000 were issued. **$250-$350**
2. 2nd class World War II solid silver, screwback version, 1943-1945. Over 950,000 were issued. **$85-$115**

Right bottom: These versions of the Order of the Patriotic War were awarded to surviving veterans on the 40th Anniversary of the Victory of the 'Great Patriotic War' in 1985.
1. 1st class 1985 gold plated version. **$45-$65**
2. 2nd class 1985 silver version. **$35-$55**

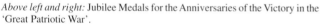

Above left and right: Jubilee Medals for the Anniversaries of the Victory in the 'Great Patriotic War'.

1. 20th Anniversary, 1945-1965. *Text on back*: Twenty Years of Victory in the 'Great Patriotic War' 1945-1965. **$20-$30**

2. 30th Anniversary, 1945-1975. *Text on back*: (a) Participation in the War XXX Years of Victory in the Great Patriotic War 1941-1945. **$20-$30** (b) Participation on the Labour Front XXX Years of Victory in the 'Great Patriotic War' 1941-1945.

3. 40th Anniversary, 1945-1985. *Text on back*: (a) Participation in the War 40 Years of Victory in the 'Great Patriotic War' 1941-1945. (b) Participation on the Labour Front 40 Years of Victory in the Great Patriotic War 1941-1945. **$20-$30**

Below left: Military Medal for the Victory Over Germany in the 'Great Patriotic War' 1941-1945. **$25-$35**

Awarded to military servicemen of the Red Army, Navy, NKVD and civilians for participation in action on the battlefronts during the 'Great Patriotic War'. Instituted May 9, 1945 and over 14,900,000 were issued.

Text on front: Our Cause is Just

We Were Victorious

Text on back: For the Victory Over Germany In the Great Patriotic War 1941-1945.

Below right: Labour Medal for the Victory Over Germany in the Great Patriotic War 1941-1945. **$25-$35**

Awarded to civilians who contributed to the victory over Germany with their efforts in labour during the 'Great Patriotic War'. Instituted June 6, 1945 and over 16,000,000 were issued.

Text on front: Our Cause is Just. We Were Victorious

Text on back: For Valiant Labour In the Great Patriotic War 1941-1945.

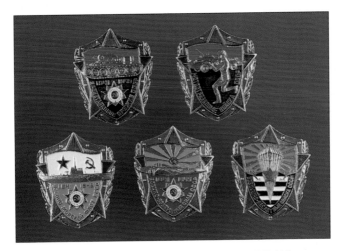

Soviet Military Forces Commemorative Pin Set, c. 1980s. **$10-$15**
1. Armoured Tank Weapons USSR 1941-1945.
2. Motor-Rifle Troops USSR.
3. Military-Sea (Navy) Fleet USSR 1941-1945.
4. Military-Air Forces USSR 1941-1945.
5. Airborne Troops USSR.

Right: 25th Year of the Victory Over Germany 1945-1970 Veterans Badge, c. 1970. **$20-$30**

Below: 30th Year of the Victory in World War II Commemorative Pins, c. 1975. **$10-$15**

1945 Victory Over Germany Commemorative Pins, c. 1970s-1980s. **$10-$15**

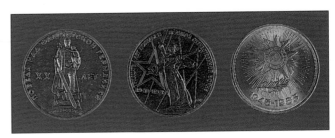

One Ruble Coins Commemorating the Victory Over Germany in the 'Great Patriotic War'.
1. 20th Year Victory Over Fascist Germany, coin issued 1965. **$10-$15**
2. Thirtieth Year Victory in the Great Patriotic War 1941-1945, coin issued 1975. **$10-$15**
3. Order of the Patriotic War 1945-1985, coin issued 1985. **$10-$15**

It was after the 'Great Patriotic War' in February 1948, that the Workers' and Peasants' Red Army was re-named the Soviet Army.

At the end of the 'Great Patriotic War' the Soviet Union had an immense military force which occupied much of Eastern Europe. The Soviet Union used its military forces to maintain control of its satellite countries in Eastern Europe. Following the war Stalin used the satellite countries as a 'buffer-zone' against possible future attacks from the countries of Western Europe. In the post-1945 era after World War II, there was no conflict between the United States, its Western Allies, and the Soviet Union. What eventually developed was an intense diplomatic and economic struggle between the two superpowers which became known as the 'Cold War'. A military alliance of seven Eastern European communist countries was formed with the USSR to counter the threat against them from the West. On May 14, 1955, the Warsaw Treaty of Friendship, Cooperation, and Mutual Assistance was signed in Warsaw, Poland creating the Warsaw Pact. Albania, Bulgaria, Czechoslovakia, East Germany, Hungary, Poland and Romania all joined the alliance. The USSR maintained strict control over the other countries in the pact and the Supreme Commander of the Warsaw Pact was from the USSR.

By the mid-1950s, the Soviet Union developed and added tactical nuclear weapons and surface-to-air missiles (SAM) to their arsenals. Under Nikita Khrushchev during the years 1955

Below: Warsaw Pact Northern Group of Forces Award Banner, c. 1950s-1960s. **$1250-$1450**
Velvet, 65" x 50".
Slogans on front -
Top: Workers of All Countries, Unite!
Bottom: Under the Leadership of the CPSU – Forward, to the Victory of Communism!

40th Year of the Victory in World War II Commemorative Pins, c. 1985. **$10-$15**

Left: 45th Year of the Victory in World War II Commemorative Pin, c. 1990. **$10-$15**

Right: Excellence in the Workers' and Peasants' Red Army (RKKA) Award Badge, c. 1930s-1940s. **$85-$95**

Text on back-
Top: The Headquarters of the Political Administration The Association of the Trade Unions for the Northern Group of Forces.
Bottom: Winner in a Socialist Competition.
Note: The Soviet forces deployed in the Warsaw Pact were comprised of four 'Groups of Forces' based in East Germany, Poland, Czechoslovakia, and Hungary. The Northern Group of Forces were based in Poland.

Soviet Military Forces Commemorative Pins, c. 1970s-1980s. **$10-$15 each**
1. Glory Soviet Army.
2. Glory Soviet Tank Forces.
3. Glory Artillery Troops.
4. Glory Railway Troops.
5. Glory Soviet Rocket Forces.
6. Glory Soviet Signals Troops.
7. Glory Soviet Navy USSR.
8. Glory Soviet Submariners.
9. Glory Soviet Airmen.
10. Glory Soviet Air Defence Forces.
11. Glory Soviet Airborne Troops.

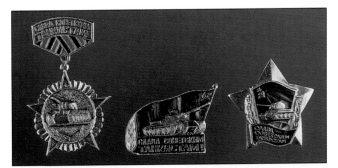

to 1964, long-range ballistic missiles and bombers carrying nuclear weapons became the main focus of the Soviet Military inventory. The Soviet Union used its nuclear capability to achieve its political goals during the 'Cold War'.

The post-war years saw great advancement in Soviet industry which supplied the Soviet Armed Forces. The Soviet Army grew with more modern tanks and formidable equipment. By the mid-1960s under the leadership of Leonid Brezhnev, the Soviets started to build-up their conventional ground forces. As a consequence of the United States involvement in Vietnam and the declining relations between the Soviet Union and China, the Soviets could foresee the possibility in being drawn into a conventional armed conflict. The Soviets also believed that a possible war in Europe, might start initially at least, using conventional warfare. The Soviet Army started to take on an ever increasing role in the military and grew considerably during this period.

The Ground Forces of the Soviet Army fell into four categories: motorized infantry, tank and airborne troops; missile troops and field artillery; engineer, signals and chemical troops; transport, medical, traffic control and police, etc. Even as there was great advances in modern weapons technology, the Sovi-

Soviet Naval Ensigns. **$65-$155**
Above: 1. silk.
Left: 2. bunting.

ets still considered the tank as one of the most important weapons in their military arsenal. The Soviets maintained that using large tank formations, the Soviet Army could penetrate deep into the enemy lines. By the mid-1980s, the Soviet Army had the world's largest tank fleet with an estimated 50,000 tanks of various models at its disposal.

The Soviet Union had two other well-armed ground forces which were independent of the Army. The Ministry of the Interior (MVD) with approximately 260,000 internal security troops and the Committee for State Security (KGB) with another 240,000 Border Guards. The MVD maintained internal law and order and controlled the Militia (Civil Police), the GAI (State Automobile Inspectorate) and the fire departments. The internal security troops maintained the prisons and the labour camps (GULAG) and guarded important State installations. During a war the MVD would have the task of securing the rear of field armies and running PoW camps. The KGB was

Left: Soviet Naval Jack, bunting. **$65-$155**

responsible to the highest echelons of the Communist Party. The KGB Border Guards patrolled the entire border of the Soviet Union and guarded every border point. The KGB security troops guarded important governmental installations, nuclear plants and Strategic Rocket Forces installations and provided a secure high-level communications network for the armed forces and for the leadership of the Communist Party. The KGB also had a coast guard with many fast missile-armed patrol boats guarding its coastal waters.

During the Civil War, Soviet Russia was attacked by the Western Powers using amphibious landings. The Bolsheviks became aware of their vulnerability to this new threat. To counter this the Soviet Navy started to implement the use of submarines, torpedo boats and mines to protect its coastline. It was only until the early 1930s that the Soviets were able to begin construction of large submarines, torpedo boats and destroyers. Construction of Navy ships and submarines were integrated into the Five-Year Plans. During the first Five-Year Plan (1928-1932), top priority was given to the building of submarines and by the third Five-Year Plan (1938-1942), ship building was given a higher priority.

During the 1950s, the Soviet Navy enjoyed a steady growth of modern surface ships of various categories as well as a large number of submarines. During the 1950s, the Soviets built their first post-war medium-range, diesel-electric propulsion, patrol submarine the 1,300-ton 'Whiskey' class which went into service. Its successor was the larger long-range 2,300-ton 'Zulu' class submarine and it was the most advanced submarine at that time. Surface ship production accelerated with the 3,100-ton 'Skory' class destroyer which was the first post-war destroyer built by the Soviet Union. Its successor was the 3,600-ton 'Kotlin' class destroyer. It was during this period that the Soviet Navy introduced the use of long-range heavy-bomber aircraft such as the Tupolev Tu-95 'Bear' and Myasishchev M-4 'Bison' which gave Naval Aviation long-range reconnaissance and strike capability.

In January 1956, Admiral Gorshkov became the head and architect of the modern Soviet Navy after Stalin's death. He pledged to build 'a powerful ocean-going navy', which would be a 'balanced fleet' having influence around the world. Between the years 1958 and 1963, the Soviet Navy introduced their first nuclear-powered submarine the 5,000-ton 'November' class submarine. The submarine was a nuclear attack submarine with an armament of twelve torpedo tubes. In July 1962, the 'November' class Leninskii Komsomol became the first Soviet submarine to surface at the North Pole. Nuclear-powered submarine development accelerated during the 1960s.

Left: VMF (Navy) USSR Pin, c. 1970s-1980s. **$10-$15**

Right: Glory VMF (Navy) Pin, c. 1970s-1980s. **$10-$15**

Left: XXV Years 1986 of the 'November' Class Nuclear Submarine Commemorative Badge. **$15-$20**

Right: 1961-1986 Jubilee of Formation 'November' Class Submarine Commemorative Badge. **$15-$20**

Left: 1961-1991 30th Year of the 'November' Class Nuclear Submarine Commemorative Badge. **$15-$25**

Right: 30th Year of the "Leninskii Komsomol" Cruise to the North Pole Commemorative Badge. This 'November' class nuclear submarine was the first Soviet submarine to surface at the North Pole. **$15-$20**

By the mid-1960s, the Soviet Navy acquired the 9,300-ton 'Yankee' class large nuclear-powered submarine (SSBN). It was equipped with 16x SS-N-6 missiles, as strategic nuclear strike missions became the primary goal of the Soviet Navy. The SS-N-6 surface-to-surface missile had a range of over 1,800 miles. During the 1970s, the impressive 'Delta' class nuclear-powered ballistic missile submarine (SSBN) went into service.

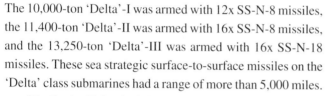

Left: 1960-1990 Nuclear-Powered Ballistic Missile Submarine (SSBN) Commemorative Badge. **$15-$20**

Right: 10th Year of the 'Yankee' Class SSBN during the 60th Anniversary of the Great October Revolution Commemorative Badge. **$15-$20**

Left: XX Years of the 'Yankee' Class SSBN Commemorative Badge. **$15-$20**

Right: 20th Year of the 'Yankee' Class SSBN "Leninets" Submarine Commemorative Badge. **$15-$20**

The 10,000-ton 'Delta'-I was armed with 12x SS-N-8 missiles, the 11,400-ton 'Delta'-II was armed with 16x SS-N-8 missiles, and the 13,250-ton 'Delta'-III was armed with 16x SS-N-18 missiles. These sea strategic surface-to-surface missiles on the 'Delta' class submarines had a range of more than 5,000 miles.

The Soviet Union had the largest fleet of surface warships in the world. In the 1960s, the Soviets built their first dedicated Rocket Cruiser the 5,700-ton 'Kynda' class cruiser used for anti-ship warfare. It carried 8x SS-N-3 missile launchers with a range of 170nm. Its successor was the 7,500-ton 'Kresta-I' class cruiser which carried 4x SS-N-3 missile launchers with one Kamov Ka-25 'Hormone-B' guidance helicopter.

In the mid-1960s, as a result of the US Navy's Polaris nuclear-powered submarines (SSBN), the Soviet Navy started to concentrate on a massive programme of anti-submarine construction. The 4,500-ton 'Kashin' class cruiser was dedicated to anti-submarine warfare (ASW) with 2x RBU 6000 and 2x RBU 1000 mortar launchers and five torpedo tubes. The 7,500-ton 'Kresta-I' Rocket Cruiser was modified for the ASW role and became the 'Kresta-II' and was fitted with 8x SS-N-14

anti-submarine missiles accompanying its mortar launchers and torpedo tubes. The 'Kresta- II' class ships carried the Ka-25 'Hormone-A' helicopter for the anti-submarine role. By the 1970s, the impressive 9,500-ton 'Kara' class cruiser was put into service and was a more advanced development of the 'Kresta-II' with increased anti-submarine and anti-aircraft armament. All of the above ASW ships also had anti-aircraft warfare (AAW) capability using surface-to-air missile launchers. There were also many diesel and nuclear-powered submarines built during this period dedicated to anti-ship and anti-submarine operations.

Also during the mid-1960s, the modern Soviet Navy incorporated anti-submarine aircraft carriers. The 18,000-ton 'Moskva' class ships carried eighteen Kamov Ka-25 'Hormone' helicopters for anti-submarine surveillance. By the mid-1970s, the much larger 42,000-ton 'Kiev' class ships carried up to thirteen Yakovlev Yak-38 'Forger' VTOL fighter-jet aircraft and approximately twenty-one Kamov Ka-25 'Hormone' helicopters. These large ships were unique, as they also had a full compliment of armaments for anti-submarine, anti-ship and anti-

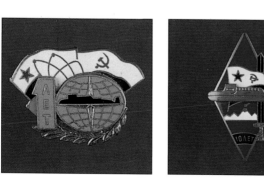

Left: 10th Year of the 'Delta' Class SSBN Commemorative Badge. **$15-$20**

Right: 10th Year of the 'Delta' Class SSBN Commemorative Badge. **$15-$20**

Left: 20th Year 1971-1991 of the 'Delta' Class SSBN Commemorative Badge. **$15-$20**

Right: XXVI Congress of the CPSU 'Delta' Class Submarine Commemorative Badge. **$15-$20**

Left: 1974-1984 'Delta' Class Submarine Service in the Arctic, Atlantic, Indian, Pacific Oceans Commemorative Badge. **$15-$20**

Right: 25th Year of the "Grozny", the First 'Kynda' Class Rocket Cruiser (RKR) Commemorative Badge. **$15-$25**

Left: "Varyag" 'Kynda' Class Rocket Cruiser Commissioned 1965 Commemorative Badge. **$15-$20**

Right: 40th Year of the Anti-Submarine (DPK) Surface Ships Commemorative Badge. **$15-$20**

aircraft warfare. The magnificent 'Kiev' class ships were decommissioned after the break-up of the Soviet Union due to their immense operating costs.

During the 1980s, the Soviet Navy commissioned some extraordinarily impressive warships and submarines to complete its 'balanced fleet' programme. The first to appear was the most impressively armed surface ship in the world, the 23,000-ton nuclear-powered 'Kirov' class Battle Cruiser. The ship's abundant array of armaments gave it the capability for all modes of warfare. It carried 20x SS-NX-20 SSM launch tubes; 12x SA-N-6 SAM vertical launch silos; 2x SA-N-4 point defence systems; 2x SS-N-14 ASW missile launchers; plus anti-submarine mortar launchers. In addition the ship had three Ka-25 'Hormone-A' ASW and possibly two Ka-25 'Hormone-B' guidance helicopters. Shortly thereafter the Soviet Navy introduced the more specialized 12,500-ton 'Slava' class cruiser and the 7600-ton 'Sovremenny' class destroyer, which were primarily configured for the anti-ship role. Also introduced was the 6,700-ton 'Udaloy' class destroyer configured primarily for the anti-submarine role. All of these three classes of modern surface ships carried the new Kamov Ka-27 'Helix' anti-submarine and guidance helicopters. During this period the largest submarine ever built anywhere in the world went into service, the gigantic 25,000-ton 'Typhoon' class SSBN submarine. It was armed with 20x SS-NX-20 nuclear missiles for strategic nuclear strike missions.

The Soviet Navy was comprised of four fleets each having its own Commander-in-Chief who was subordinate to the Admiral of the Fleet of the Soviet Union. The Baltic Fleet at Baltiysk, was primarily a coastal defence force. By the 1980s, it had fourteen submarines and 252 surface warships. The Northern Fleet based at Severomorsk had the most ocean-going ASW units and the latest nuclear submarines as the port

Above left: 1991 Anti-Submarine Warfare (DPLK) Commemorative Badge. **$15-$20**

Above right: 20th Year of the "Admiral Isakov" 'Kresta-II' Class Cruiser Commemorative Badge. **$15-$20**

Right: "Kerch" 'Kara' Class Cruiser Badge. **$15-$20**

Aircraft Carrier Badges. **$15-$20 each**
1. Heavy Cruiser Kiev.
2. Heavy Cruiser Minsk.
3. Heavy Cruiser Baku.

had unrestricted access to the open seas and the Atlantic Ocean. By the 1980s, it had 149 submarines (forty-nine were SSBN), one aircraft carrier, and 152 surface warships. The Black Sea Fleet at Sevastopol, also patrolled the waters of the Mediterranean Sea. By the 1980s, it had forty-two submarines, two air-

Left: "Otlichniy" 'Sovremenny' Class Destroyer Badge. **$15-$25**

Right: 5 Years "Otlichniy" 'Sovremenny' Class Destroyer of the Northern Fleet Badge. **$15-$20**

Left: Northern Fleet Badge. **$15-$20**

Right: Submariner of the Northern Fleet Badge. **$15-$20**

Left: Northern Fleet Submariner Badge. **$15-$20**

Right: 1982 Northern Fleet Submarine (Delta) Service Badge. **$15-$20**

Left: 20th Year of Formation of the Northern Fleet 1971-1991 Commemorative Badge. **$15-$20**

Right: XXV Years of the Squadron of Surface Ships of the Northern Fleet Badge. **$15-$20**

Left: XXV Years of the Northern Fleet Submarine Service Commemorative Badge. **$15-$20**

Right: XXV Years of the Northern Fleet Submarine Service Commemorative Badge. **$15-$20**

Left: 1933-1988 Northern Fleet Commemorative Badge. **$15-$20**

Right: 50th Year of the Northern Fleet Commemorative Badge. **$15-$20**

Right: 60th Year of the Northern Fleet Commemorative Badge. **$15-$20**

Far right: XV Years 1991 Delta Submarine of the Northern Fleet Badge. **$15-$20**

Soviet Navy Chief of Staff Flags. **$65-$155**
1. Chief of Staff of the Soviet Navy, one stripe, bunting.
2. Chief of Staff of the Soviet Armed Forces, two stripes, silk.

Soviet Navy Supreme Commander (Ministry of Defence) Flags. **$65-$155**
1. Supreme Commander of the Soviet Navy, one stripe, bunting.
2. Supreme Commander of the Soviet Armed Forces, two stripes, silk.

Soviet Navy Commander Flags. **$65-$155**
1. Formation Commander, one star, bunting.
2. Flotilla or Squadron Commander, two stars, bunting.
3. Fleet Commander, three stars, bunting.

craft carriers, and 286 surface warships. The Pacific Fleet at Vladivostok, sailed the Pacific and Indian Oceans. By the 1980s, it had 110 submarines (twenty-four were SSBN), one aircraft carrier, and 259 surface warships. The surface warships deployed in the naval fleets included cruisers, destroyers, frigates, and other light forces.

The Soviet Navy had the largest fleet of warships in the world. The immense variety of surface warships and submarines gave the Soviet Navy a highly capable 'balanced fleet', which made its presence felt in every ocean of the world to support the political interests of the USSR.

The Soviet Air Force at its inception was designed to provide tactical support for the Ground Forces of the Red Army. The Soviet Red Army Commander maintained operational control of the Air Force through the Military District Commanders. From the period 1928 to the outbreak of World War II, the Soviet Air Force grew substantially with fighters and light-bomber aircraft designed to perform tactical air support missions. During World War II the Soviet Union continued to use the Air Force in direct support of the Red Army's ground forces.

The famous Ilyushin Il-2 'Shturmovik' ground attack and anti-tank aircraft was used extensively during World War II to support the Red Army's ground forces. The Il-2 holds the record to this day, as being the aircraft produced in the greatest quantity ever. During the war the Soviets were producing 1,200 Il-2's per month. By the end of the war over 36,000 Il-2's were manufactured. The Il-2 was instrumental in the Soviets victory over Germany as it inflicted heavy damage to the German tank formations along the eastern front. The Il-2 had over 1,500 lbs. of steel armour plating protecting the cockpit and its 1,600 hp twelve-cylinder Mikulin AM-38 engine from ground fire. A second crew member at the rear of the cockpit manned an anti-aircraft gun to protect the aircraft from aerial attacks from the rear. The Il-2 carried a large complement of armaments. It had four forward facing wing mounted guns and under-wing hard points for up to eight rocket missiles and 1,000 lbs. of bombs. There was also an internal weapons bay that could hold 1,250 lbs. of anti-armour bombs.

The Soviet Air Force was usually used in the support of the Army or Navy but after World War II it eventually became a separate entity having aircraft allocated for the Air Defence Command, Air Transport Command, and for Long-Range Aviation.

After the war the Soviet Air Force started to concentrate on the development of fighter-jet interceptor aircraft. The MiG-15, 17, 19, 21 series were small maneuverable jet fighters which

Soviet Navy Formation Pennants. **$65-$155**
1. White, bunting, 48" x 9".
2. Red, bunting, 95" x 7 1/2".

Soviet Air Force Flag, bunting. **$150-$200**

From the Air Force of the USSR Pin, c. 1970s-1980s. **$15-$25**

were designed to provide point air defence against localized air strikes.

The Sukhoi Su-7 'Fitter' and Yakovlev Yak-28 'Brewer' jet fighter-bombers were also developed. The Su-7 was a close support strike fighter which had an excellent high speed, low altitude stable platform for clear weather weapons delivery. The Su-7 was designed around the massive 22,000 lbs. thrust Lyulka AL-7F afterburning turbojet engine which was one of the largest turbojet engines built during that time period. The Yak-28 had two wing mounted 13,000 lbs. Tumansky R-11 afterburning turbojets which allowed for an internal weapons bay that could carry up to 4,500 lbs. of bombs designed for tactical nuclear strikes. To facilitate this the Yak-28 had a glazed nose for a navigator/bombardier compartment. Due to the versatility of the aircraft's layout there were also reconnaissance, electronic countermeasures (ECM) and fighter-interceptor variants of the Yak-28 produced.

The Mikoyan-Gurevich (MiG) design bureau built a world-renowned line of fighters for the Soviet Air Force. The MiG design bureau built over 10,000 MiG-21 'Fishbed' fighters of all variants, which made it the most produced modern fighter-jet ever built. By the mid-1980s, the MiG-21 had served in thirty-seven air forces throughout the world making it the most widely used jet fighter in history. The initial variants of the MiG-21 were lightly armed day fighters of limited range. The MiG-21 (MF variant) was a supersonic, single-pilot fighter jet capable of Mach 1.06 at low level and Mach 2.1 at high altitude. It had a tailed-delta plan form with its engine inlet air intake at the nose of the fuselage. Over a period of more than twenty years, the MiG-21 was produced in more variants than any other fighter jet ever built. Improvements to its avionics, weapon's systems, range and all-weather capability, made the MiG-21 the backbone of Soviet tactical air power for many, many years.

The physical appearance of the fighter changed remarkably over the years as improvements were made to enhance its capabilities. The MiG-21PF was the first variant of the initial version the MiG-21F. The MiG-21PF had an increased diameter engine inlet to facilitate the up-rated Tumansky R-11F afterburning turbojet engine of 13,700 lbs. thrust, a larger radome, and an enlarged dorsal spine just aft of the cockpit holding additional fuel. The next version was the MiG-21PFM, which had the new sideways-hinged canopy and an increase in the chord of the vertical tail. The version that followed was the MiG-21PFMA, which had an enlarged dorsal spine over the full-length of the upper fuselage. The MiG-21MF was generally similar to the PFMA but internally it had a Tumanskii R-13-300 afterburning turbojet engine of 14,500 lbs. thrust and the canopy incorporated a rear-view mirror. The most striking in appearance was the MiG-21SMT, which had an even larger dorsal spine over the full-length of the upper fuselage holding even more fuel. The final version was the MiG-21bis developed in the late 1970s, which introduced the latest avionics and had a more advanced version of the Tumanskii afterburning turbojet, the R-25 of 16,500 lbs. thrust. There were also two-seat trainer versions, variants built for reconnaissance and for export.

Mikoyan-Gurevich (MiG) Design Bureau Pin Set with plastic case, c. 1980s. **$25-$35**

By the late 1960s, the Soviet Air Force needed a successor for the MiG-21 to modernize its jet fighter fleet. A multi-role fighter with greater range, good airfield performance, excellent air superiority, advanced radar and weapons systems was needed. The Mikoyan-Gurevich design bureau developed the MiG-23 'Flogger'. It was a single-pilot, variable-geometry fighter with the large 25,350 lbs. R-29B Tumansky afterburning turbofan engine. Its variable-geometry wing gave the fighter good low speed airfield performance when the wings were swept forward and also provided the fighter with excellent high speed air-combat capabilities when the wings were swept backward. The variable-geometry wing allowed the same basic airframe to be designed for the interceptor/air superiority role, as well as a dedicated ground-attack aircraft. To enhance its maneuverability the MiG-23 had horizontal tail surfaces known as 'tailerons', when driven together provided pitch control and differentially provided roll control. The nose of the fighter was fitted with a large radar and the engine air intakes were positioned on either side of the aircraft's fuselage. The MiG-23 was capable of Mach 1.2 at low level and Mach 2.35 at high altitude. The MiG-27 was a modified version of the MiG-23 being designed for the ground-attack role. It had a distinctive redesigned wedge-shaped 'duck-nose' for better pilot visibility and modified engine and air intakes for low altitude flight. The multi-role MiG-23 'Flogger' became the most numerous combat aircraft in service with the Soviet Air Force with production exceeding 600 units per year.

The MiG-25 'Foxbat' actually went into service well before the MiG-23 even though it has a higher designator number. In the late 1950s, the Soviet Union was threatened by the USAF B-70 high altitude Mach 3 bomber and reconnaissance

1/48th Scale Models of Variations of the MiG-21, c. 1980s.
These kits were manufactured by OEZ, Czechoslovakia.
1. MiG-21PFMA.
2. MiG-21MF.
3. MiG-21SMT.
4. MiG-21bis.
5. MiG-21bis export version (Finnish Air Force).

aircraft. The Mikoyan-Gurevich design bureau was given the task to build an interceptor capable of shooting down the B-70. The B-70 project was subsequently canceled but the Soviets continued the development and production of the MiG-25 noticing its great potential as a high altitude interceptor and reconnaissance aircraft. It required Soviet ingenuity to develop such a remarkable jet fighter capable of flying at greater than Mach 3 at altitudes of up to 100,000 feet with the technology available at that time in the Soviet Union.

The MiG-25 was the first jet fighter having two vertical tails which eventually became the trend for future modern fighters that were eventually developed in the West. The two vertical tails were required to maintain directional control of the aircraft at high supersonic airspeeds. In order to withstand the extremely high surface temperatures the airframe would be subjected to while flying at Mach 3, the aircraft had to be made of a weldable low-grade stainless steel alloy. The reason for this was because the airframe consisted mainly of fabricated steel sections that were welded together allowing the airframe to expand and contract with changes in temperature. The leading edges were made of titanium to withstand the most ex-

treme temperatures, while the surfaces which were not subjected to high surface heating were made of aluminum.

To power this remarkable aircraft unique engines had to be developed. The 27,000 lbs. thrust Tumansky R-31 afterburning engines functioned as 'turbo-ramjets'. The MiG-25 had two of these simply configured but powerful engines. The R-31 was a single-shaft engine with a five-stage compressor driven by a single-stage turbine. At takeoff and at low altitudes and airspeeds, the engines were very inefficient burning enormous amounts of fuel to achieve the required thrust. The engines were designed to be efficient at high altitudes and airspeeds which was the regime the MiG-25 was designed to be most effective. The large air intakes, the most complicated in design at that time, were designed to capture a large amount of

Aviation History USSR MiG-23 and MiG-27 Commemorative Pins.

air and increase the pressure of the air entering the engine optimizing the engine's high Mach performance. The most powerful radar at that time was built for the MiG-25, the 600 kW 'Fox Fire'. It was designed to burn through enemy jamming and had a range of over 50 miles. It was so powerful that if it was left on while taxiing it could kill a rabbit at 3000 feet. In conjunction with the 'Fox Fire' radar, the MiG-25 was equipped with the largest air-to-air missiles in the world the AA-6 'Acrid'. With 4x 'Acrid' AAM's attached to its wings the MiG-25 could fly at a maximum altitude of approximately 88,000 feet at a maximum speed of Mach 2.83. In the clean configuration without missiles, the MiG-25 could fly at speeds up to Mach 3.2. It was a remarkable straight-line interceptor which was of such concern to the US that they had to design the F-15 to counter it. It becomes obvious that the F-15's general configuration resembles that of the MiG-25.

During the mid-1950s, Long-Range Aviation grew with the advent of the Tupolev Tu-16 'Badger' and the supersonic Tu-22 'Blinder' medium-bombers. Intercontinental nuclear delivery capability was achieved with the development of the large Tu-95 'Bear' and Myasishchyev M-4 'Bison' long-range bombers.

The large and impressive Tu-95 'Bear' bomber was the solution for the Soviet's requirement for an intercontinental long-range aircraft capable of carrying a heavy load of free-fall bombs.

The jet engine technology available in the mid-1950s, did not have the efficiency for very long-range aircraft as they burned too much fuel. In order to overcome this obstacle, the Soviets designed the largest turboprop engine ever built to achieve their goal. The engine was the 12,000 ehp Kuznetsov NK-12M turboprop driving two large four-blade counter-rotating propellers of 18 feet 4 inches in diameter. Even to this day, it is a remarkable accomplishment for a gearbox to be designed and capable of absorbing 12,000 shaft horsepower. These Soviet engines of the 1950s were the forerunners of the 'prop-fan' technology of today. The four massive engines propelled the Tu-95 to airspeeds of up to 540 mph normally reserved for jet airplanes. As a result of these high airspeeds the Tu-95 was the only turboprop having such highly swept-wings characteristic of jet airplanes. The Tu-95 had a range of 7,800 miles carrying 25,000 lbs. of weapons. It was also designed for the reconnaissance role capable of loitering at maximum endurance speeds for up to 28 hours.

The Soviet Air Force continued to modernize its bomber fleet over the decades. By the late 1970s, the Soviets intro-

Aviation USSR Tu-16 1952 Commemorative Pin. **$5-$10**

MiG-29 Commemorative Pins. **$5-$10**

Left: MiG-29 Lapel Pins. **$5-$10**
Right: Su-27 1978 Commemorative Pin. **$5-$15**

duced the Tu-26 'Backfire' bomber. It had variable-geometry wings and was powered by two large 45,000 lbs. of thrust NK-144 afterburning turbofans. The large bomber had a range of approximately 7,500 miles cruising at long-range cruise of Mach .8 with its wings swept in the mid-position. With the wings swept fully back the Tu-26 could fly at a maximum speed of Mach 2. The successor to the 'Backfire' bomber was the even larger Tu-160 'Blackjack'. It also utilized variable-geometry wings and was powered by four uprated NK-144D afterburning turbofans.

The Soviet Air force also modernized their fleet of jet fighters in the 1980s by introducing the agile MiG-29 'Fulcrum' and the formidable and larger Su-27 'Flanker'. The MiG-31 'Foxhound' which was derived from the MiG-25 became the Soviet Air Force's new long-range interceptor. The dreaded Su-24 'Fencer' was a modern interdictor and deep strike fighter. All of these modern aircraft had the most advanced avionics and weapons systems available which made them formidable adversaries.

The modern Soviet Air Force was comprised of five major elements:

1. Frontal Aviation – Its primary role was air support for the Soviet Army's Ground Forces. It had more than 5,000 aircraft of which 4,000 were in service with the Warsaw Pact opposing NATO. It was equipped with fighters for counter-air operations; ground- attack for close air support of ground troops; strike aircraft for interdiction missions; reconnaissance aircraft; tactical air transport aircraft and helicopters to provide air mobility of the ground forces; armed helicopters for anti-tank operations; electronic countermeasures (ECM) aircraft. Frontal Aviation used the MiG-15, 17, 19, 21, 23, 25, 27, 29, Su-7, 17, 24, 27 fighter jets; Yak-28, Il-28, Su-25 fighter-bombers; Mil-4, 6, 8, 24, 26 helicopters.

2. Long-Range Aviation – Its role was to provide strategic bombing capability (nuclear or conventional) using free-fall bombs or air-to-surface missiles of medium and long-range targets; aerial tankers for in-flight refueling; reconnaissance and ECM. The service was equipped with more than a 1,000 aircraft. Long-Range Aviation used the Tu-16, 22 medium-bombers; Tu-95, 26, 160, M-4 long-range bombers.

3. Military Air Transport – The service consisted of more than 1,600 aircraft and 2,000 helicopters. They provided freight and troop-carrying capabilities. Military Air Transport used the An-12, 22, 24, Il-18, 76 transport aircraft; Mil-4, 6, 8, 10, 26 helicopters.

4. Naval Aviation – This service supported the Navy providing long-range reconnaissance, bombers carrying conventional or nuclear air-to-surface missiles, and anti-submarine warfare. The force had more than 1,200 aircraft and approximately 250 helicopters. The Yak-38 'Forger' VTOL jet fighter was used on the 'Kiev' large aircraft carriers with the Ka-25 'Hormone' helicopter. Naval Aviation used the Tu-16, 95, 22, 26, Il-38 aircraft.

5. National Air Defence Command – In 1954, an independent service called 'PVO Strany' was created to defend the Soviet Union against Western armed nuclear bombers. This service protected military targets and industrial complexes in the Soviet Union. The PVO had four major air

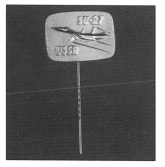

Left: Su-27 USSR Lapel Pin. **$5-$10**

Right: Mikoyan Design Bureau MiG-31 Commemorative Pin. **$5-$10**

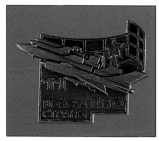

Left: Long-Range Aviation (Tu-160) Badge. **$20-$30**

Right: Anti-Aircraft Defence Forces of the Country (PVO) Badge, c. 1980s. **$45-$65**

Left: XXX Years of the Fighter Aviation Regiment PVO Commemorative Badge. **$20-$30**
Right: 50th Year of the Armed Forces of the PVO 1941-1991 Commemorative Badge. **$20-$30**

arms: interceptors, surface-to-air missiles, warning and control systems, and anti-space defense troops. The service maintained more than 2,600 interceptors, 5,000 radar installations, and some 50,000 surface-to-air missiles at over 1,000 missile sites throughout the USSR. The National Air Defence Command used the following Yak-28,

Tu-28, 126 (AWACS), Su-9/11, 15, 27, MiG-21, 23, 25, 29, 31 interceptors.

During the era of the Soviet Union it was essential for it to build-up a large and powerful military machine to protect itself from the capitalist countries of the West. At that time, a defeat for the Soviets would have meant a loss of all that they have struggled for since the creation of the world's first socialist state, the USSR.

USSR Ministry of Defence Military I.D. Booklet (unissued), c. 1980s. **$10-$15**

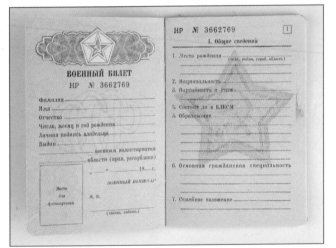

Soviet Military Poster, "Plakat" Publishers Moscow, c. 1988. **$25-$35**
Text on top: For Our Soviet Homeland!
Title: Technology – for Reliable Hands!
Text on front: New Technology – High Level of Mastering
Collective Weapons – Personal Responsibility
Always in Battle Readiness
Classes – Index of Mastering.

Right: Military Officer of the Ministry of Defence USSR I.D. Booklet (unissued), c. 1980s. **$10-$15**

USSR Ministry of Defence Award Document (unissued), c. 1980s. **$10-$15**
Text on front: Our Slogan Must Be One – To Diligently Learn the Military's Business ... V.I. Lenin

Military Oath Document (unissued). **$10-$15**
"Plakat" Publishers Moscow, c. 1989.
Text on front -
Top: Ready to Defend the Homeland!
Bottom: Homeland, Party Oath!
Text on back -
Top: I, a citizen of the Union of Soviet Socialist Republics, join the troops of the armed forces of the USSR, take the oath and solemnly swear to be honest, brave, disciplined, vigilant warrior, strictly keeping military and state secrets, observe the constitution of the USSR and Soviet laws, unquestionably fulfill all military regulations and orders of the commanders and chiefs.

I swear to conscientiously study military affairs, in every possible way guard military and national property and till the last breath be loyal to the nation, to the Soviet homeland and to the government.

I am always ready by the order of the Soviet government to step forth and defend my homeland – Union of Soviet Socialist Republics and, being a warrior of the armed forces of the USSR, I sear to defend it courageously, skillfully, with dignity and honour, with no mercy for my blood and life to achieve full victory over the enemy.

If I break my solemn oath, then I shall receive severe punishment by Soviet law, collective hatred and contempt by the Soviet nation.
Bottom: Dear ... We Congratulate You with this emotional event of Your life – accepting the Military oath. From this day on You are a trustworthy defender of the socialist Fatherland. Remember this always and be proud of this!

The Solemn promise of loyalty to your nation, your Homeland – is an important lawful and military-political act, which obligates You invariably and with all responsibility to fulfill the precepts of V.I. Lenin, the demands of the Communist party, Soviet government to the armed defenders. You know, that the world is now uneasy. The interests of security of our country, complicated international atmosphere require from You the highest political vigilance, readiness with weapon in your hands at any minute to step forth to defend the historic socialist conquest.

Carry the high honour and dignity of the soviet warrior – warrior-patriot, warrior-internationalist. Piously respect the military exploits of the older generations. Be on the same level as the heroes, learn from them courage and love of the Fatherland, loyalty to the ideals of communism.

Commander of the Military Unit
Secretary of the Party Committee (Party Bureau)
Assistant of the Political Unit
Commander Secretary of the Committee VLKSM

Order of the Red Banner.
Awarded to personnel of the Soviet Armed Forces, KGB, and MVD Border Guards and Internal Troops for acts of courage in the defence of the socialist homeland.
Instituted August 1, 1924 and over 600,000 were issued.
1. World War II version on ribbon suspension, c. 1943-1950s. **$65-$95**
Over 300,000 were issued during World War II.
2. Post-World War II version, c. 1950s-1980s. **$45-$75**
Text on front: Workers of All Countries, Unite!

Left: Order of the Red Star.
Awarded to personnel of the Soviet Armed Forces, KGB, and MVD Border Guards and Internal Troops for outstanding achievements in the defence of the USSR in war and peace. Instituted April 6, 1930 and over 4,000,000 were issued.
1. World War II version. Over 2,800,000 were issued during World War II. **$65-$85**
2. Final post-World War II version. **$45-$65**
Text on front: Workers of All Countries, Unite!

Medals for Irreproachable Service in the Armed Forces of the USSR. Instituted September 14, 1957.
1. 10 years. **$20-$30**
2. 15 years. **$20-$30**
3. 20 years. **$20-$30**

Medal for 100th Anniversary of Lenin's Birth. **$25-$40**
Awarded for Military Valour. Instituted November 5, 1969 and approximately 1,000,000 were issued.
Text on back: For Military Valour On the Commemoration of the 100th Year Anniversary of the Birth of V.I. Lenin.

Medal for Distinction in Military Service.
Awarded to personnel of the Soviet Armed Forces and Border Guard Troops for excellence in training and courage in active service. Instituted October 28, 1974.
1. 1st class, over 30,000 were issued. **$55-$75**
2. 2nd class, over 120,000 were issued. **$45-$65**

Right: Order for Service to the Homeland in the Armed Forces of the USSR. **$250-$350**
Awarded to personnel of the Soviet Armed Forces, KGB and MVD Border Guards and Internal Troops for excellence in training and outstanding services in the military. Instituted October 28, 1974. Can be awarded in 1st, 2nd and 3rd classes. 1st class over 10 were issued; 2nd class over 500 were issued; 3rd class over 75,000 were issued.
1. 3rd class.

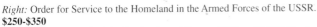

Excellence in the Soviet Army (for enlisted men) Proficiency Badges.
1. c. 1950s (screwback). **$25-$35**
2. c. 1950s (pin back). **$25-$35**
3. c. 1960s (2 versions). **$20-$25**
4. c. 1970s-1980s. **$15-$20**

1st Class Tankist Badge, c. 1950s. **$55-$75**
There are also badges for Master to 3rd class.

Combined Armed Specialist (for officers) Badges, c. 1960s-1980s.
1. Master. **$15-$20**
2. 1st class. **$15-$20**
3. 2nd class. **$15-$20**
4. 3rd class. **$15-$20**

Soviet Army (for enlisted men) Specialist Badges. **$15-$20**
1. Master, brass pin back, c. 1960s.
2. 1st class, brass screwback, c. 1960s.
3. 2nd class, brass screwback, c. 1960s.
4. 3rd class, brass screwback, c. 1960s.

World War II Excellence in the Soviet Army (for enlisted men) Proficiency
Badges, c. 1942-1955.
1. Excellent Tankist. **$65-$85**
2. Excellent Artillerist. **$65-$85**
3. Excellent Firefighter. **$65-$85**

Elite Guards Badge, c. 1970s-1980s.
$15-$25

Soviet Army Armour Sleeve Insignia. **$10-$15**

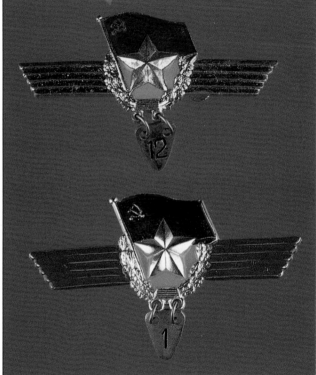

Soviet Army Extended Services Badges.
1. c. 1950s-1960s. **$20-$25**
2. c. 1970s-1980s. **$15-$20**

Soviet Army Motor-Rifle Troops Sleeve Insignia.

Soviet Military Police Patrol Breast
Badge, c. 1980s. **$25-$35**

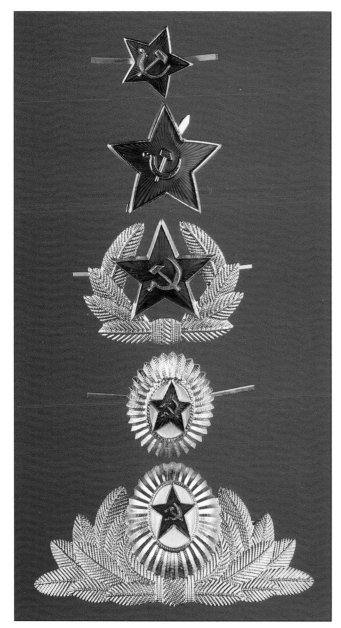

Military Officer's School Graduation Badges. Intermediate level military school for Lieutenant ranks, etc.
1. c. 1960s-1970s. **$35-$45**
2. c. 1980s. **$20-$25**

Left: Military Academy Graduation Badge, c. 1970s-1980s. High ranking officer's school for Captains, Majors etc. **$20-$25**
Right: General Staff Academy Graduation Badge, c. 1980s. Highest ranking officer's school for Colonels, Generals etc. **$20-$25**

Soviet Army Cap Badges, c. 1970s-1980s.
1. Enlisted Man's Beret and Cadet's Peaked Cap Badge. **$10-$15**
2. Enlisted Man's Fur Hat Cap Badge. **$15-$20**
3. Enlisted Man's Peaked and Ensign's Beret Cap Badge. **$10-$15**
4. Marshal's, General's and Officer's Peaked Cap and Fur Hat Cap Badge. **$10-$15**
5. Officer's Parade Peaked Cap Badge. **$15-$20**

Suvorov Junior Military Academy Graduation Badges, 1970s-1980s.
1. Suvorov Military Academy (SVU). **$15-$20**
2. Leningrad SVU. **$20-$25**

Left: Military Political Academy (VPA) in the Name of Lenin Graduation Badge, c. 1970s-1980s. **$20-$25**

Right: Military College (VU) Graduation Badge, c. 1950s. **$35-$55**

Excellence in the VMF Soviet Navy (for enlisted men) Proficiency Badges.
1. c. 1930s. **$85-$125**
2. c. 1950s-1960s. **$20-$25**
3. c. 1970s-1980s. **$15-$20**

Soviet Navy Officer's Surface Ship Badges, c. 1960s-1980s.
1. Admiral. **$25-$35**
2. Captain. **$25-$35**

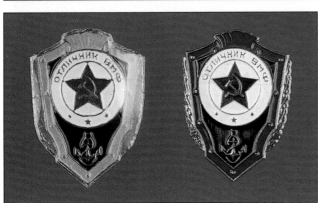

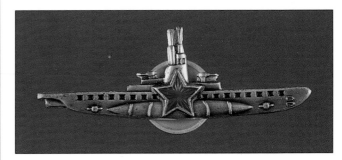

Soviet Navy Officer's Submarine Badges.
1. Admiral, c. 1950s-1970s. **$25-$35**
2. Captain, c. 1950s-1970s. **$25-$35**
3. Captain, c. 1980s. **$15-$20**

Nuclear-Powered Ballistic Missile Submarine (SSBN) Serviceman's Badge, c. 1970s-1980s. **$20-$30**

Soviet Naval Aviation Officer's Badge, c. 1980s. **$25-$35**

Soviet Navy Extended Services Badge, c. 1950s-1960s. **$20-$25**

Soviet Navy Officer's Cap Badges, c. 1970s-1980s.
1. Admiral. **$10-$15**
2. Captain. **$10-$15**

Left: Soviet Navy Enlisted Man's 'Donald Duck' Cap Badge, c. 1970s-1980s.
$10-$15

Right: Soviet Naval Infantry Beret Cap Badge, c. 1970s-1980s. **$10-$15**

Above, below left, and below:
For a Long Cruise Award Badges.
1. Surface Ship, 1961 type. **$15-$20**
2. Submarine (diesel), 1961 type. **$15-$20**
3. Submarine (nuclear), 1961 type. **$15-$20**
4. Surface Ship "Ochakov". **$15-$20**
5. Surface Ship and Submarine, 1976 type (small variant). **$15-$25**
6. Surface Ship and Submarine, 1976 type (large variant). **$15-$20**

Submarine Year of Service Badges. **$15-$20**

Veteran Submariner Badges.
1. Diesel. **$15-$20**
2. Nuclear. **$15-$20**
3. 1918-1978 60th Anniversary of the
Soviet Military Forces. **$15-$25**

'In Remembrance of Service' Soviet Navy Badges.
1. Surface Ship. **$15-$25**
2. Submarine. **$15-$20**

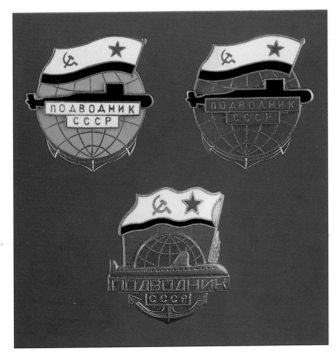

Submariner of the USSR Badges. **$15-$20**

Left: 1971-1981 'Charlie' Class Nuclear Cruise Missile Submarine Commemorate Badge. **$15-$20**

Right: 1971-1981 Dolphin Squadron Commemorative Badge. **$15-$20**

Left: 1977 Dolphin Squadron Commemorative Badge. **$15-$20**

Right: Pacific Fleet Participation in the Transition with the Northern Fleet Badge. **$15-$20**

Left: 75th Year of the "Pantera" Squadron Commemorative Badge. **$15-$20**

Right and below: For Transition Over the Equator Badges.
1. Soviet Navy Surface Ship. **$15-$20**
2. Minsk. **$20-$30**
3. Novorossisk. **$20-$30**
4. Baku. **$20-$30**

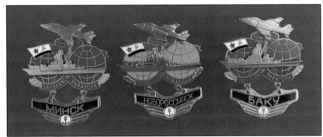

Soviet Navy Submarine Commemorative Badges during the 50th Year of the USSR (1972). **$15-$20**
1. 10 years 'APL'.
2. 15 years 'APL'.

"Leningradskii Komsomolets" 'Krivak-I' Class Pin. **$10-$15**

Left: "Admiral Kuznetsov" Aircraft Carrier Badge. **$15-$20**

Right: For Honour and Courage for Service on the "Storozhevoi" 'Krivak-I' Class Frigate Badge. **$15-$20**

Left: X Years of the "Aquamarine" 1980 Commemorative Badge. **$20-$30**

Right: XXX Years of the "Komsomolets" Destroyer Commemorative Badge. **$15-$20**

Komsomol Submarine Service Badge. **$15-$20**

60th Year of Patronage of the Komsomol (VLKSM) with the Soviet Navy Submarine Service Commemorative Badge. **$15-$20**

Left: XX Years of Formation SSBN Commemorative Pin. **$10-$15**

10 Years of Service with the Soviet Navy Nuclear Submarine Fleet Badge. **$15-$20**

Right: 40th Year of Naval Aviation Pacific Fleet Commemorative Pin. **$10-$15**

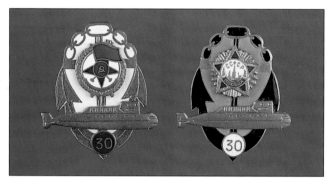

Left: 50th Year of Soviet Naval Aviation (Beriev Be-12) Commemorative Pin. **$10-$15**

Right: 50th Year 'SRS' Soviet Navy Commemorative Pin. **$10-$15**

30th Year (1975) of the 'Great Patriotic War' (WW II) 'Delta' Class Submarine Commemorative Badges.
1. Order of the Red Banner. **$15-$20**
2. Order of Victory. **$15-$20**

Left: Soviet Navy Rocket Cruiser Pin. **$10-$15**

Right: Murmansk Sea Port Badge. **$20-$30**

Merchant Fleet Flags of the Soviet Union, bunting. **$65-$155**
1. 30" x 60".
2. 96" x 48".

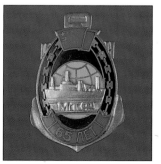

Left: Naval Order of Lenin Commemorative Badge. **$20-$30**

Right: 65th Year of the Navy's Merchant Fleet (MTF) Commemorative Badge. **$20-$30**

Russian Soviet Federated Socialist Republic (RSFSR) Merchant Fleet Flag, bunting. **$65-$155**

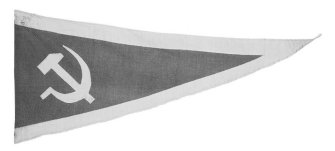

Soviet Naval Pennants, bunting. **$65-$155**
1. 60" x 25".
2. 96" x 48".

Soviet Military Flag Finials. **$25-$35**
1. Aluminum.
2. Steel.

Left: Red Banner Baltic Fleet (DKBF) Badge. **$15-$20**

Right: XV Year of the Red Banner Fleet. **$15-$20**

Left: Sevastopol Black Sea Fleet Badge. **$15-$20**

Right: 1940-1975 Maksim Gorkii Commemorative Badge. **$15-$20**

Soviet Navy Training Ship Badges. **$15-$20**
1. Smolny.
2. Khasan.

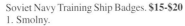

Left: 50th Year of the 'Spetsnaz' VMF Soviet Navy's Special Units Commemorative Badge. **$20-$30**

50th Year 1938-1988 of the 1st Guards Regiment Veterans (GMTAP) Commemorative Badge. **$20-$25**

Right: 1918-1988 Veteran of Soviet Naval Aviation Order of Lenin (EVVAUL) Commemorative Badge. **$20-$25**

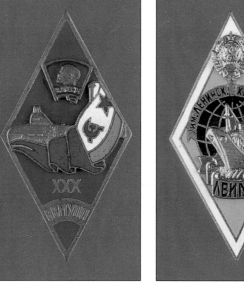

Left: 30th Year of the Soviet Navy Submarine Commemorative Pin. **$10-$15**

Right: XXX Years of the Komsomol (VLKSM) Higher Military Navy Academy Submarine Navigation (VVMUPP) Commemorative Badge. **$25-$35**

Left: Leninsk Komsomol Military Engineering Naval Academy (LVIMU) Graduation Badge. **$25-$35**

Right: Class of 1981 Special Navy Command (Officers) Submarine Academy (VOKVMF) Graduation Badge. **$20-$30**

Right: Murmansk Military Engineering Naval Academy (MVIMU) Graduation Badge. **$25-$35**

Right center: Murmansk Naval Academy (MMU) Graduation Badge. **$15-$25**

Far right: 50th Year 1941-1991 of the M.V. Frunze Higher Military Naval Command (Officers) Academy (VVMKU) Commemorative Badge. **$25-$35**

Left: 1933-1978 Popov Higher Military Naval Academy Reconnaissance (BBMURE) Commemorative Badge. **$15-$20**

Right: '80' S.M. Kirov Command (Officers) Academy of Submarine Mine Warfare (UKOPP) Badge. **$15-$20**

Left: Nakhimov Military Naval Academy (NVMU) Badge. **$15-$20**

Right: Soviet Navy Command (Officers) Higher Military Naval Academy (KVVMU) Graduation Badge. **$20-$25**

1917-1987 Higher Military Naval Submarine Academy (VVMPU) Commemorative Badge. **$20-$25**

Left: V.I. Lenin Higher Military Naval Engineering Academy (VVMIU) Graduation Badge, c. 1970s-1980s. **$20-$25**
Center: Higher Military Naval Academy (VVMU) Submarine Navigation Graduation Badge, c. 1970s-1980s. **$20-$25**
Right: Soviet Naval Academy Graduation Badge, c. 1970s-1980s. **$20-$25**

Excellence in the VVS Soviet Air Force (for enlisted men) Proficiency Badges.
1. c. 1950s-1960s. **$20-$25**
2. c. 1970s-1980s. **$15-$20**

WW II Excellence in the Soviet Air Force (for enlisted men) Proficiency Badges, c. 1942-1955. (two versions) **$65-$85**

Left: WW II Excellence in the PVO Anti-Aircraft Defence Forces (for enlisted men) Proficiency Badge, c. 1942-1955. **$65-$85**

Right: Excellence in the Local Anti-Aircraft Defence Forces (MPVO) of the USSR Badge, c. 1950s-1960s. **$35-$45**

Soviet Air Force Pilot's Wings, c. 1966 type. **$20-$35 each**
1. 1st class.
2. 2nd class.
3. 3rd class.
4. Basic.

Soviet Air Force Navigator's Wings, c. 1966 type. **$20-$35 each**
1. 1st class.
2. 2nd class.
3. 3rd class.

Air Force Extended Services Badge, c. 1950s-1960s. **$20-$25**

Soviet Air Force Veteran Navigator
Badge, c. 1960s-1970s. **$45-$55**

Soviet Air Force 'Sniper' Wings, c. 1970s. **$20-$35 each**
1. Pilot-Sniper Wing.
2. Navigator-Sniper Wing.

Soviet Air Force Sleeve Insignia.

Soviet Air Force Marshal's, General's and Officer's Peaked Hat Cap Badge
with Wing Badge on Crown, c. 1970s-1980s. **$10-$15**

Excellence in the Airborne Troops (for
enlisted men) Proficiency Badge,
1970s-1980s. **$15-$20**

Paratroopers Badges, c. 1970s-1980s. **$15-$25 each**
1. Basic (plus pendant).
2. 10 jumps (plus pendant).
3. Excellent Parachutist, 10 jumps (plus pendant).
4. Excellent Parachutist, 50 jumps (plus pendant).
5. Instructor Parachutist, 100 jumps (plus pendant).
6. Instructor Parachutist, 500 jumps (plus pendant).
7. Instructor Parachutist, 1000 jumps (plus pendant).

Airborne Troops Sleeve Insignia.

60th Year 1990 of the Airborne Troops Commemorative Pin. **$10-$15**

Left: Airborne Troops Military College Graduation Badge, c. 1950s. **$35-$55**

Right: 60th Year of the Soviet Parachutists of the USSR Commemorative Badge. **$25-$35**

50th Anniversary of the October Revolution 1917-1967 Military/Political Award Banner, c. 1967. **$850-$1250**
Velvet, 65" x 50".
Text on front -
Slogan top right: For Our Soviet Homeland!
Text top left: Central Committee of the CPSU
Presidium of the Supreme Soviet USSR Council of Ministers USSR.
Bottom: For Achieving High Marks in Military and Political Exercises in Honour of the 50th Year of the Great October Socialist Revolution.

Left: For Participation in a Military Parade Commemorative Badge, c. 1970s-1980s. **$10-$15**

Right: Order of the Red Banner Pin, c. 1970s-1980s. **$10-$15**

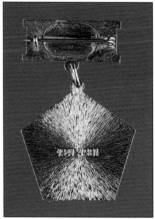

40th Year of the Red Banner Aviation of the Southeast 1941-1981 Commemorative Badge. **$25-$35**

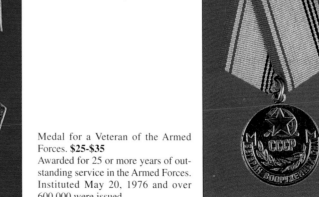

Above: Elite Guards of the "Vilenskii" Aviation Regiment Commemorative Pin. **$10-$15**

Right: 40th Year 1941-1981 of the "Pomeranskii" Institute of Aviation Industry Commemorative Badge. **$25-$40**

Medal for a Veteran of the Armed Forces. **$25-$35**
Awarded for 25 or more years of outstanding service in the Armed Forces. Instituted May 20, 1976 and over 600,000 were issued.

Left: Soviet War Veteran Commemorative Pin, c. 1970s-1980s. **$5-$10**

Right: Elite Guards 1941-1945 World War II Commemorative Badge. **$25-$40**

Left: In Remembrance of the Armed Forces of the USSR on the 50th Year of Military Service Commemorative Badge. **$25-$35**

Right: 25th Anniversary of the Battle for Moscow Commemorative Pin, c. 1966. **$5-$10**

WW II 'Great Patriotic War' Battle Commemorative Pins, c. 1980s. **$10-$15**
1. Battle of Moscow 1941-1942.
2. Stalingrad's Battle 1942-1943.
3. Battle for Leningrad 1941-1944.

Three Ruble Commemorative Coin, coin issued 1991. **$15-$20**
Text on front: 50th Year of the Destruction of the Fascist Germans During the Battle of Moscow 1941-1991.

Voluntary Society for the Contribution to the Army, Air Force and Navy (DOSAAF) Badges.
1. For Active Work in DOSAAF Training, c. 1950s-1960s. **$25-$35**
2. DOSAAF Instructor's Badge, c. 1950s-1960s. **$35-$45**
The DOSAAF was a government sponsored nationwide organization formed in 1951 to provide physical fitness for preparedness for the Soviet Military. Other technically oriented hobbies were also provided for children and teenagers through a network of regional clubs throughout the USSR.

Ready for Labour and Defence (GTO) Campaign Award Badges.
1. c. 1930s-1940s. **$35-$55**
2. c. 1970s. **$10-$15**
3. Ready to Defend Our Homeland Pin, c. 1970s. **$10-$15**
The Ready for Labour and Defence (GTO) Campaign was instituted in 1931 by the Soviet Government to strengthen the Soviet people through Physical Culture (sports). It was designed to provide support for the Soviet Military and to provide a more capable labour force for industry. The national sports campaign was also designed to improve the 'Soviet' man through physical fitness thus preventing absenteeism, drunkenness, and hooliganism within the population.

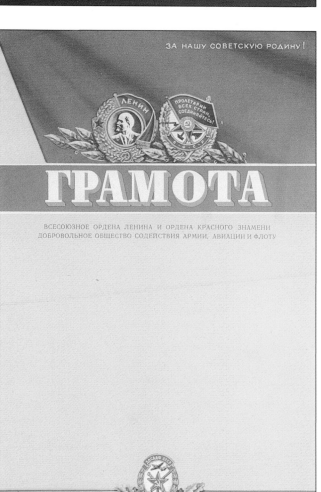

DOSAAF Award Document (unissued), c. 1970s-1980s. **$10-$15**
Text: For Our Soviet Homeland!
AWARD DOCUMENT
All-Union Order of Lenin and Order of the Red Banner
Voluntary Society for the Contribution to the Army, Air Force and Navy.

EIGHT

THE SOVIET SPACE PROGRAM

It was Konstantin Tsiolkovsky the great Russian scientist who was the first to come out with workable plans for man's conquest into space. Tsiolkovsky in 1883, suggested using the principle of reactive motion for creating interplanetary vehicles and found a number of important engineering solutions for rocket design. He envisioned the rocket as the means of overcoming gravity and charted the course that would be taken by many of his disciples and followers.

The first research and development team working on rocket engines and rockets in the Soviet Union was the Gas Dynamics Laboratory (GDL) in Leningrad. It was a State sponsored organization established in 1921.

On October 1931, Sergei Korolev met Fridrikh Tsander and together formed the Group for the Study of Reactive Motion (GIRD) which was based in Moscow. Korolev became the head of the group and in 1933, GIRD created and launched the first Soviet propelled rocket GIRD-09 that August. Late in 1933, GIRD and the Gas Dynamics Laboratory (GDL) merged into the world's first State owned Rocket Research Institute dedicated to the research of rocket technology. Korolev was appointed its deputy director for science and in early 1934, became the head of the rocket vehicle department. Between the years of 1946 and 1956 after years of research and development, Korolev's teams produced several types of single-stage missiles with ranges from 300 to 1200 kilometers. By 1954, an intercontinental ballistic missile programme was underway in the Soviet Union and involved a number of research institutes, design offices, and factories. By 1957, the world's first intercontinental ballistic missile flew successfully and its name was the R-7 ICBM.

S.P. Korolev USSR 1906-1966 Commemorative Medal, c. 1980s. **$45-$65**

It took Soviet ingenuity to develop a rocket that could produce a total thrust reaching 1,000,000 lbs., which was unprecedented for that time period, using the technology that was available in 1950s. In order to accomplish this engineering achievement the R-7 had a central core with four strap-on boosters. There were four thrust-chambers (nozzles) in the central core and in each of the four strap-on boosters, resulting in a total of twenty main nozzles at the rocket's base. In addition to the main nozzles there were four attitude control nozzles on the central core and two attitude control nozzles on each of the strap-on boosters. The end result was the R-7 rocket actually having thirty-two nozzles firing at the same time at lift-off! To enhance the rocket's reliability the central core and each strap-on booster had only one turbo-pump assembly feeding the propellants to the four thrust-chambers and the attitude control nozzles at its base.

This remarkable ingenuity of clustering the four thrust-chambers was required as a result of the metallurgical technology available at that time. The strap-on booster engine with the two attitude control nozzles was called the RD-107, which developed 228,480 lbs. of thrust in vacuum and the central core's engine with four attitude control nozzles was called the RD-108. The RD-108 was very similar in design to the RD-107 and developed 215,040 lbs. of thrust in vacuum. To develop one very large thrust-chamber that could produce over 200,000 lbs. of thrust and able to withstand such high temperatures, pressures and mass flows would have been taxing at that time. So in order to overcome this difficulty, four thrust-chambers each providing approximately 55,000 lbs. of thrust were grouped together, being fed by one turbo-pump assembly became the obvious solution. At lift-off the R-7 produced a total thrust of 928,000 lbs., a remarkable accomplishment for its time. Variants of this same rocket developed in the 1950s, are still being used today to launch satellites into Earth orbit, space probes to the planets, and Soyuz manned spacecraft and Progress supply ships to the space station Mir.

It was on January 30, 1956, that the decision was made to launch a satellite into orbit around the Earth in the following year using the R-7 ICBM which was currently under development. It was on October 4, 1957 (forty years after the 'Great October Socialist Revolution') that the world's first satellite was launched into space. The satellite named Sputnik was a 23 inch diameter sphere weighing 184 lbs. which had four whip antennae protruding at its side in a 'swept-back' position. Inside the sphere there were two radio transmitters which emitted the famous 'beeps' heard around the world from space ushering in the space age. Other 'firsts' would continue to flow out of the USSR in the quest to explore space.

On November 3, 1957, Sputnik 2 carried the dog Laika which was the first living creature to be launched into space. Physiological parameters such as pulse, respiration, blood pressure and movement were monitored. During Laika's stay in space she did not exhibit any adverse effects of weightlessness

XXV Year of the Baikonur Cosmodrome Commemorative Medal. **$45-$65**
Text on back: Here is the Genius of the Soviet People that Commenced the Daring Storming of Space 1955-1980.

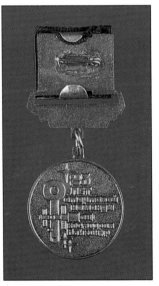

25th Year 1957-1982 of the Baikonur Cosmodrome Commemorative Medal. **$45-$65**
Text on back: 25th Year of the Launch Team at the Baikonur Cosmodrome.

or from the environment of space. Soviet scientists were greatly encouraged and began plans to send a man into space. Sputnik 2 had no re-entry capability and after seven days in space an automatic system put Laika to sleep ending the life of the world's first space traveler.

On May 15, 1958, Sputnik 3 was the first scientific laboratory sent into space to conduct complex geophysical research. One of the most important results was the discovery of the Earth's radiation belts. The satellite continued to send data to earth for some two years.

In the year 1959, the Soviets concentrated their efforts on sending probes to the moon and the Luna programme was cre-

RD-107 and RD-108 engine cluster at the base of the R-7 ICBM (Vostok) launch vehicle.

4 October 1957 USSR Sputnik Commemorative Medal. **$45-$65**
Text on back: First in the World to Launch an Artificial Satellite from the Earth.

XXX Years Anniversary of Sputnik Commemorative Medal, c. 1987. **$45-$65**
Text on back: Here is the Genius of the Soviet People that has Commenced the Daring Storming of Space.

ated having a series of 'firsts' as well. On January 2, 1959, Luna 1 was the first probe to reach the earth's escape velocity and thirty-four hours after launch it flew past the moon by less than 3700 miles. Luna 2 was launched on September 12, 1959, and two days later on September 14, 1959, Luna 2 was the first space probe to reach the surface of the moon delivering memorial pendants of the Coat-of-Arms of the USSR. On October 4, 1959, Luna 3 was launched and on October 7, 1959, it photographed the far side of the moon which is not seen from the earth. After processing the film the pictures were transmitted to the earth by the spacecraft's television system. Luna 3 made the first experiment of studying another celestial body by means of a spacecraft.

The new decade was approaching and in conjunction with the Luna programme the Soviets were preparing to send a man in space for the first time. There were seven precursor flights to test the Vostok spacecraft before it could be used for a manned flight. The most notable of the Vostok precursor flights was the flight of Spaceship-Satellite 2 on August 19, 1960, which was the fourth flight in the series and conducted the first return of living animals from space. Two dogs Belka and Strelka returned safely after one day in space. Three additional flights were carried out and the last precursor flight took place on March 25, 1961, in order to approve the Vostok spacecraft for manned flight.

It was on the morning of April 12, 1961, at 0907 local time that the first manned spacecraft was launched from the Baikonur Cosmodrome with cosmonaut Yuri Gagarin on board. The rocket was a variant of the R-7 launch vehicle called Vostok. The Vostok launch vehicle had an additional upper-stage with

Right: Sputnik Commemorative Pins. **$5-$10**

Below: Laika First Passenger on a Sputnik Commemorative Pin. **$20-$30**

Below right: Luna 1959 USSR Commemorative Pin. **$15-$25**

Yuri Gagarin 12 April 1961 Bronze Table Medallion. **$80-$95**
Text on back: In Honour of the World's First Flight of a Human Being into Space.

One Ruble Coin Commemorating the 20th Anniversary of Man in Space, coin issued 1981. **$10-$15**
Text on front: 1961 1981
20th Year of the First Flight of a Man in Space Yu.A. Gagarin.

Yuri Gagarin Year of Birth and Death Commemorative Medal. **$45-$65**
Text on back: Federation of Cosmonautics USSR
The First Cosmonaut of the Planet Earth Yuri Alekseevich Gagarin 1934-1968.

25th Anniversary of Man in Space Commemorative Medal.
Text on front: 25th Year of the Flight of Man in Space **$45-$65**
Text on back: 12 April 1961
The Launch of the Spaceship with Y.A. Gagarin.

50th Anniversary of the Birth of Yuri Gagarin Commemorative Medal. **$45-$65**
Text on back: Federation of Cosmonautics USSR First Cosmonaut of the Planet Earth Yuri Alekseevich Gagarin
1934-1984.

Right: XXX Years Anniversary of the Flight of Yuri Gagarin Commemorative Medal. **$45-$65**
Text on back: XXX Years of the Flight of Yuri Gagarin
12 April 1961
12 April 1991
Federation of Cosmonautics USSR Medal.

a single thrust-chamber producing 12,000 lbs. of thrust that would propel the Vostok spacecraft into orbit. The Vostok spacecraft made one complete orbit of the Earth lasting 108 minutes.

It required Soviet ingenuity, using the technology available at that time, to design the 10,400 lbs. Vostok spacecraft that Yuri Gagarin orbited the Earth in. The spacecraft had two main sections, a spherical 7.5 feet diameter re-entry capsule and an instrument module which included a retro-rocket system. The spacecraft had a conventional internal nitrogen-oxygen atmosphere at a normal atmospheric pressure for the cosmonaut which was supplied by a collar of compressed air bottles mounted externally on the instrument module. The re-entry capsule had an ablative shield covering its entire surface to protect it against the frictional heating of re-entry. The ablative shield was then covered with metal foil reflecting the solar heat away from the spacecraft while it was in orbit.

Orientation of the spacecraft for re-entry which required the retro-rocket to face in the same direction of flight and at a precise angle, was accomplished automatically by steering jets fed from compressed gas storage bottles. The spacecraft was maneuvered to an attitude which was determined by two externally mounted solar sensors, stopping the maneuver when they were facing the sun. As a back-up, the cosmonaut could manually orient the spacecraft using a 'vzor' optical orientation device using the Earth's horizon as a reference. On the main instrument panel there was a rotating globe which showed the position of the spacecraft at all times over the Earth and could be used by the cosmonaut to manually fire the retro-rocket at the precise position over the Earth for re-entry. As a further back-up, if the retro-rocket failed to fire, the spacecraft's orbit would decay within ten days and the spacecraft would re-enter the Earth's atmosphere automatically. This is why the spacecraft had enough provisions for ten days in orbit.

The re-entry capsule itself was a sphere which did not require stabilizing attitude jets on the capsule during re-entry. Orientation of the capsule was achieved by the simple procedure of off-setting the center-of-gravity of the sphere. As gravitational forces and air pressure built up, the spherical capsule would swing around to the proper attitude, which would allow the cosmonaut to receive the re-entry deceleration G-forces in the approved 'chest-to-back' position. To simplify the re-entry procedure even further, the capsule re-entered along a truly ballistic trajectory requiring the cosmonaut to be subjected to eight to nine 'G's' during the re-entry phase.

The Soviet spacecraft returned to the Earth on land in the confines of the USSR instead of on the waters of the oceans to

XXX Years Anniversary of the Flight of Yuri Gagarin Commemorative Medal. **$45-$65**
Text on front: 12 April 1961
Baikonur Cosmodrome
Text on back: XXX Years of the Flight of Yuri Gagarin 12 April 1961 - 12 April 1991.

Yuri Gagarin Commemorative Pins. **$10-$15**

maintain the security of its space programme. The USSR had an extremely large vacant land area available which allowed the space capsule to land without undue risk to populated areas. The cosmonaut was sitting on an ejection seat using aneroid pressure sensors which would sense the increasing pressure as the capsule descended through the atmosphere. At approximately 23,000 feet the ejection seat rockets would fire ejecting the cosmonaut from the capsule. At approximately 13,000 feet the cosmonaut's parachute system would deploy bringing him safely to the Earth as a conventional parachutist. The re-entry capsule's parachute system would also deploy at approximately 13,000 feet bringing it safely to the Earth as well. The cosmonaut could stay in the capsule for the entire flight until touchdown on the Earth's surface as a back-up. It is believed that Gagarin did this on his flight, though the Soviets have never issued this information for sure. In addition, this ejection system could also be used if a malfunction occurred during the launch phase of flight propelling the cosmonaut safely away from the launch vehicle.

The following series of Vostok flights were of increasing duration and also produced the first multi-day group flights in which two spacecraft were in orbit at the same time coming to within three miles of each other.

The last Vostok spacecraft in the series was Vostok 6 which heralded another first for the Soviet Union. On June 16, 1963, Valentina Tereshkova was the first woman to be launched into space. Her flight on Vostok 6 lasted just shy of three days. This last flight in the Vostok series marked the first stage in the development of manned Earth orbiting spacecraft in the USSR.

The next manned Soviet spacecraft was called the Voskhod which was a variant of the former Vostok. It was designed to hold multi-man crews but still utilized the 7.5 feet spherical capsule which externally was the same as the Vostok. The Voskhod's internal arrangement however was different and the cosmonauts did not wear space suits for the purpose of conserving space. On October 12, 1964, Voskhod 1 was launched carrying three men into space for a one-day mission. The Voskhod had a unique feature when compared to the Vostok, as it had a soft-landing rocket system since the cosmonauts could not eject out of the capsule during the return to Earth.

It was four months later that another Soviet 'first' would be accomplished using the Voskhod spacecraft. On March 18, 1965, Pavel Belyayev and Alexei Leonov were launched into space aboard Voskhod 2. It was on this mission that Alexei Leonov became the first man to walk in space. The Voskhod spacecraft had attached to its hull an 'accordion' style cylindrical airlock that would extend outward as air pressure was supplied to it. The Voskhod interior was not designed for the temperatures and vacuum of space so an airlock was required. When the pressure in the airlock and the capsule were the same, Leonov would then open the specially added hatch and enter into the airlock. The hatch of the capsule was then closed and sealed. Gradually the pressure within the airlock was lowered to the vacuum of space. Then Leonov opened the hatch of the airlock and begin his walk in space. Leonov spent twenty minutes in the conditions of space, twelve of which he was floating freely in space attached to the ship by means of a tether.

1/25 Scale Model of the Vostok Spacecraft, c. 1980s. The kit was manufactured by VEB Plasticart, East Germany.

One Ruble Coin Commemorating Valentina Tereshkova, coin issued 1983. Commemorating the 20th Anniversary of Valentina Tereshkova's Vostok-6 Flight 16-19 June 1963.

Right: Voskhod 2 18 March 1965 Alexei Leonov First Man to Walk in Space Pin. **$10-$15**

His space suit had an independent life support system backpack. The mission ended in a safe recovery after one day in space.

Between the years 1963 and 1965 the Luna programme was in full swing as the Soviets sent Luna 5, 6, 7, and 8 to the moon in order to continue further exploration of the moon and to solve the problem of soft landing a spacecraft on the lunar surface. On January 31, 1966, Luna 9 was launched and became the first spacecraft to make a successful soft landing on the moon. On February 3, 1966, it transmitted the first panoramic pictures of the lunar landscape back to Earth.

The Voskhod programme was now complete, as it was an intermediate step leading to the next generation spacecraft Soyuz. The Soyuz spacecraft was truly a more complicated spacecraft than its predecessors as it was a mini orbital space station with much flexibility in its design. It had three sections: at the rear was the instrument and propulsion module, in the middle was the command/re-entry module, and at the front end was the orbital module. The instrument and propulsion module had the maneuvering and retro-rocket engines as well as attitude and control thrusters, which allowed the Soyuz to accomplish orbital and docking maneuvers. The Soyuz command/re-entry module was different than the sphere of the Vostok. It was 'bell-shaped' so it could adjust and flatten its reentry path aerodynamically to reduce the 'G-loads' on the cosmonauts to approximately three to four 'G's'. This would be an important consideration for long duration missions in space. The re-entry module had soft landing solid fuel retro-rockets at its base that would fire approximately three feet above the ground to slow the capsule to a gentle landing. The spherical shaped orbital module at the front end could be configured for specific scientific experiments which were to be accomplished during the mission. It acted as an airlock during space walks and it also could be fitted with a docking mechanism at its front end. Also notable are the green thermal blankets that cover the spacecraft protecting it from the sun's radiation and the large solar panels attached to the instrument module that provide the spacecraft with electricity for long duration flights.

On April 23, 1967, Soyuz 1 lifted-off from the Baikonur Cosmodrome manned by Vladimir Komarov. When the spacecraft reached orbit it developed a series of problems, one of which affected the spacecraft's attitude control. The ground controllers decided to discontinue the flight prematurely. After a successful re-entry the parachutes of the re-entry module tangled and failed killing Komarov. Unfortunately, he was the first space fatality.

It took the Soviets a year and a half to recover from the Soyuz 1 tragedy when the manned Soyuz 3 spacecraft was launched with Georgi Beregovoi on October 26, 1968. Soyuz 3 rendezvoused with the unmanned Soyuz 2, which was a rehearsal for the docking that would follow during the next Soyuz mission. The Soyuz 3 mission was accomplished successfully and Beregovoi returned safely to the earth after 4 days in space.

On January 14, 1969, Soyuz 4 was launched with one cosmonaut on board, V. Shatalov. A day later on January 15, Soyuz

1/30 Scale Model of the Soyuz Spacecraft, c. 1980s.
The kit was manufactured by the Moscow Experimental Factory "OGONEK" USSR.

5 was launched with a crew of three cosmonauts, B. Volynov, A. Yeliseyev and Ye. Khrunov. After one day in space the two Soyuz spacecraft docked creating the world's first experimental space station assembled in orbit. Cosmonauts A. Yeliseyev and Ye. Khrunov of Soyuz 5 via a thirty-seven minute space walk, transferred into Soyuz 4 joining the lone cosmonaut V. Shatalov. Both spacecraft stayed in space for three days conducting scientific experiments and observations and then successfully returned to Earth independently. This mission was a vital step for the Soviet space programme's attempt at a manned mission to the moon as this maneuver was required in the mission profile.

Unfortunately for the Soviets the N-1 moon rocket was unsuccessful. Two launch attempts during 1969 both ended in failure. The N-1 was the largest rocket ever built. It had thirty Kuznetsov NK-33 engines at its base developing an outstand

Left: Luna-16 1970 Pin. **$10-$15**

Right: 1970 Luna-17 Pin. **$10-$15**

ing 10,348,800 lbs. of thrust at lift-off! The first N-1 was launched on February 21,1969. After one minute into the launch an oxidizer line leading to one of the NK-33 engines ruptured due to excessive vibrations and an uncontrolled fire developed at the base of the first stage ending the flight. The N-1 was launched again on July 3, 1969, and this attempt failed as a piece of metal fell into the oxidizer pump of one of its engines causing the rocket to explode moments after lift-off falling back onto the launch pad. One of the main contributing factors for the failures of the N-1 was the decision by the Soviets not to build a first-stage test stand to check the thirty first-stage engines firing simultaneously. The reason for not building the test stand was due to budget and time constraints put on the N-1 moon programme. Two more launch attempts were made of the N-1, one on June 27, 1971 and the final on November 23, 1972. Both launches ended in failure and the Soviet manned lunar programme was terminated.

The unmanned Luna programme continued during the 1960s with orbiting probes and on December 24, 1966, Luna 13 (an upgraded version of Luna 9) soft landed on the moon. On September 12, 1970, Luna 16 was launched which was the first automatic lunar soil sample-return mission. It landed on the moon and drilled a core sample, which was then inserted into the spherical re-entry capsule at the top of the probe. Using an ascent module rocket and a re-entry capsule it returned a 101 grams lunar core sample back to Earth. This was the first time an unmanned space probe brought a lunar sample back to Earth automatically. On November 17, 1970, Luna 17 landed on the moon delivering the unmanned lunar rover Lunakhod 1. It traveled on the lunar surface for more than 10 months over a distance of 6.5 miles. On February 14, 1972, Luna 20 was launched and became the second successful automatic lunar soil sample-return mission. On January 8, 1973, Luna 21 was launched delivering the second lunar rover Lunakhod 2 which traveled over twenty-three miles on the lunar surface. Extensive scientific research of the moon was accomplished during the Soviet Luna programme.

In addition to the lunar exploration conducted during the 1960s and 1970s, the Soviets also sent probes to the planets Venus and Mars.

The Soviet's Venera programme was designed to conduct scientific research of the planet Venus. On February 12, 1961, Venera 1 was launched and became the first interplanetary probe to leave the Earth's orbit. The probe continued to transmit data back to Earth until February 27, 1961 from a distance of 3 million miles and then the transmissions stopped. Venera 1

eventually passed to within 60,000 miles of Venus on May 20, 1961. Venera 2 was launched on November 12, 1965 and on February 27, 1966, flew by Venus at 15,000 miles above the sunlit side of the planet's surface. Venera 3 was launched four days after Venera 2 on November 16, 1965 and on February 27, 1966, became the first probe to land on another planet. It carried a pendant with the Coat-of-Arms of the USSR. Unfortunately, Venera 3 seized transmissions prior to the probe's entry into Venus's atmosphere. Venera 4, 5, and 6 accomplished similar missions to that of Venera 3 but successfully transmitted data back to Earth during their descents through the Venusian atmosphere. After aerodynamic braking, a parachute system was deployed to provide the entry module with a slow descent through the Venusian atmosphere, while transmitting data on pressure, density, temperature and chemical composition.

Venera 7 was designed with a more advanced descent module capable of landing on the surface of Venus and transmit data back to Earth. On August 17, 1970, Venera 7 was launched and on December 15, 1970, the descent module successfully landed on the surface of Venus transmitting data back to Earth for 23 minutes. Venera 8 was launched on March 27, 1972, and it successfully landed on the sunlit side of the planet. It had increased heat protection and temperature controls to withstand the harsh environment. The following versions of the Venera probes were even more sophisticated as they were designed to study the surface of the planet and transmit TV images back to Earth. Venera 9 was launched on June 8, 1975, and after a successful landing on October 22, 1975, it transmitted back to Earth the first black and white TV panoramas of the Venusian surface for 53 minutes. On March 1, 1982, Venera 13 transmitted back to Earth the first colour TV pictures of Venus's surface and sky. It also carried a surface drill which transported the soil into the interior of the probe for analysis.

The Soviets also sent probes to Mars to study the 'red' planet. On November 1, 1962, the Mars 1 space probe was launched towards Mars. After almost five months in space at 66 million miles from Earth transmissions seized from the space probe. At that time it was the longest distance for communication between the Earth and a space probe. On May 19 and 28, 1971, the Mars 2 and Mars 3 were launched respectively. Both probes carried a descent module which in addition to scientific studies of the surface and atmosphere of the planet, had a TV system to transmit images of the planet back to Earth. Unfortunately, the Mars 2 lander failed, while the Mars 3 lander only sent back transmissions to Earth for 20 seconds after landing on the surface which may have been caused by dust storms at the landing area. However, the orbital modules continued to transmit data to Earth until the Soviets terminated the missions in August 1972. In 1973, during the Mars 'launch window' four Mars probes were launched. Mars 4 and 5 where designated orbiters while Mars 6 and 7 were equipped with descent modules. The Mars 5 spacecraft successfully achieved orbit and the Mars 6 lander transmitted data for only 148 seconds after its parachutes opened as transmissions stopped. The Mars programme was unfortunately not as successful as its counterpart the Venera programme.

During the 1970s, the Soviet manned space programme began focusing on the development of manned, long duration, earth-orbiting space stations. The purpose of these orbiting laboratories was to conduct extensive research of space technology, space biology and medicine, geophysics, astronomy and astrophysics. A series of space stations called Salyut were designed to accomplish these tasks. On April 19, 1971, Salyut 1 was launched into earth orbit by the large Proton launch vehicle. The Salyut 1 space station was 49 feet long and had a maximum diameter of over 12 1/2 feet.

On April 23, 1971, the Soyuz 10 spacecraft with three cosmonauts aboard was launched and a day later it docked with Salyut 1. Unfortunately due to a docking/hatch malfunction, the cosmonauts were unable to transfer into the space station. Design modifications were made to the docking mechanism and on June 6, 1971, Soyuz 11 was launched and after a successful docking the three cosmonauts transferred into the Salyut 1 making it the first manned orbital space station complex. The cosmonauts stayed in the Salyut 1 for twenty-three days conducting numerous scientific experiments. After a successful undocking and re-entry the Soyuz 11 crew were unexpectedly found dead in their space capsule by the recovery team following a normal touchdown. A valve malfunctioned at the moment the re-entry module separated from the orbital module of the Soyuz and all the air in their Soyuz re-entry capsule escaped into space. The cosmonauts died instantly as they were not wearing space suits. During that period of the Soviet manned space programme, the cosmonauts did not wear space suits during the launch and re-entry phases of flight. After this incident the Soyuz spacecraft was manned by only two cosmonauts both wearing space suits during the critical phases of flight.

Throughout the 1970s, seven Salyut space stations were launched alternating between civilian and military missions. Salyut 3, 4, and 5 were second-generation Salyut space stations. They were modified in having three larger rotatable so-

One Ruble Commemorative Coin, coin issued 1979.
Text on front: Games of the XXII Olympiad Moscow 1980.
Coin shows a third generation Salyut Space Station in orbit with a Soyuz and Progress Spacecraft docked at each end.

lar panels which allowed them to continuously be oriented towards the sun. The space station could therefore maintain a fixed attitude in space while orbiting the earth. This was a very useful feature when conducting scientific observations and experiments. As a consequence of the Salyut's larger solar panels the Soyuz spacecraft did not have its distinctive solar panels anymore, as it relied on internal battery power for the docking and re-entry phases of flight. The Soyuz spacecraft's batteries were recharged by the Salyut's large solar panels when it was docked. The elimination of the heavy solar panels from the Soyuz allowed it to carry more supplies and scientific equipment to the Salyut space station.

Salyut 6 and 7 were the third and last generation Salyut space stations of the series. These Salyuts were modified in having two docking ports one at each end of the space station. At the forward docking port the Soyuz ferry spacecraft would be docked and at the aft port the highly innovative Progress resupply spacecraft would dock. A Soyuz spacecraft could also dock at the aft port if required as the docking mechanisms were the same, though the Progress cargo ship had to dock at the aft port due to the plumbing for the refueling operation. The Progress cargo ships increased the operational life of the Salyut space stations to several years by transporting over 5,000 lbs. of life-support consumables and maneuvering propellants. The Progress spacecraft also functioned as a 'space-tug' using its engines to maneuver the space station to higher orbits. The Progress spacecraft was based on the design and hardware of the Soyuz. The cargo module (formerly the orbital compartment of the Soyuz) carried over 2,800 lbs. of food, water, clothing, experimental apparatus and other supplies, which would be transferred to the station by the cosmonauts. The refueling module (formerly the command module of the Soyuz) was designed to carry and automatically transfer propellants and refill the Salyut's propellant tanks. The Progress service module was similar to that of the Soyuz spacecraft. It contained systems for automatic rendezvous, docking and de-orbit. After a complete transfer of supplies and propellants, the cosmonauts would then reload the cargo module with the waste from the orbiting station. The Progress would then undock carrying the garbage to a fiery re-entry into the Earth's atmosphere.

The Salyut 6 space station was launched on September 29, 1977. Over the duration of three years, eight months the space station was manned by 33 cosmonauts and was replenished by twelve Progress cargo ships. The upgraded Soyuz T series spacecraft was first tested with the Salyut 6 space station. Its interior was re-designed to carry three cosmonauts wearing space suits. It also had improved digital avionics and the distinctive solar panels were reinstated on the Soyuz T. The Soyuz T-3 spacecraft was launched on November 27, 1980, and was the first three-man crew aboard a Soyuz spacecraft in a decade. The Soyuz 40 spacecraft was the last of the original Soyuz spacecraft to fly and was also the last mission to Salyut 6. The last crew of Soyuz 40 left the Salyut 6 space station on May 22, 1981.

Salyut 7 the last in the series of Salyut space stations was launched on April 19, 1982. Over the duration of four years two months the space station was manned by twenty-nine cosmonauts and was replenished by twelve Progress cargo ships

and two larger Cosmos 1443 and 1686 space station modules. The Soyuz T-10B crew was launched on February 8, 1984 and stayed aboard Salyut 7 for 237 days, the longest duration in the Salyut series.

Another Soviet first was accomplished by the last crew that inhabited the Salyut 7 space station. On February 20, 1986, the space station Mir was launched. The Soyuz T-15 crew was launched on March 13, 1986 and was the first crew to visit the Mir space station. On May 5, 1986, the crew made history by performing the first 'space taxi' mission. Using the Soyuz T-15 spacecraft they left the Mir space station and traveled to the Salyut 7. On June 25, 1986 after twenty days aboard the Salyut 7, they completed the final experiments and retrieved some hardware and then traveled back to the space station Mir. The cosmonauts then completed their stay in space aboard Mir and then returned to Earth on July 16, 1986. The Salyut 7's Earth orbit decayed naturally and the space station entered the Earth's atmosphere on February 7, 1991.

Much was learned in the fifteen years during the Salyut space station programme. The Soviet's goal of maintaining a permanent manned presence in space is currently being achieved with the space station Mir. Tsiolkovsky envisioned a permanent manned presence in space approximately 100 years ago and it was the Soviets who achieved it.

Right: XX Years of the Space Training Center in the Name of Y.A. Gagarin 1980 Commemorative Pin. **$15-$20**

50th Anniversary of the Birth of Yuri Gagarin Commemorative Medal. **$45-$65**
Text on back: Space Training Center 1984
In the Name of Yu. A. Gagarin.

XXV Years of the Squadron of Cosmonauts Badge. **$45-$55**
Text on back: TsPK Space Training Center In the Name of Y.A. Gagarin 1960-1985.

Space Training Center in the Name of Yu.A. Gagarin Medals. **$45-$55**
1. 1960 Star City 1980.
2. 1960 Star City 1990.

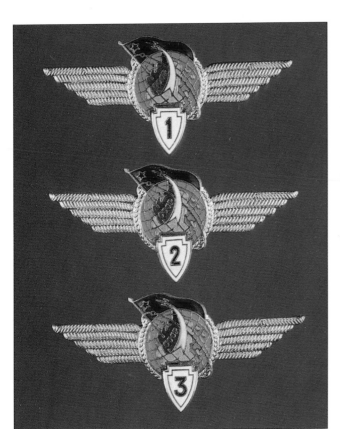
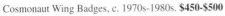

Cosmonaut Wing Badges, c. 1970s-1980s. **$450-$500**
1. 1st class.
2. 2nd class.
3. 3rd class.

Right: Pilot Cosmonaut USSR Badge, 1970s-1980s. **$65-$95**

Far right: Glory to the Soviet Cosmonauts Commemorative Pin, 1970s-1980s.
$10-$15

Right: Honoured Test Engineer of the Baikonur Cosmodrome Award Badge. **$45-$65**

Veteran of the Baikonur Cosmodrome Award Medal. **$45-$65**
Text on back: Here is the Genius of the Soviet People that has Commenced the Daring Storming of Space.

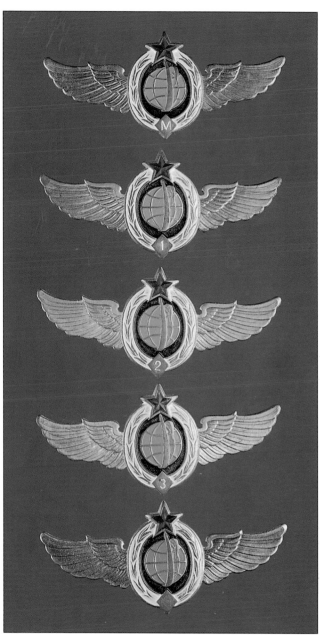

Military Space Programme (Strategic Rocket Forces) Wing Badges, c. 1989. **$75-$95**
1. Master.
2. 1st class.
3. 2nd class.
4. 3rd class.
5. Basic.

1957-1987 Cosmonautics Commemorative Pin. **$15-$25**
Text on back: XXX Years of the Cosmonautics Era.

NINE

AEROFLOT

Aeroflot, the Soviet Airlines, was the largest airline in the world during the existence of the Soviet Union. Aeroflot was the only airline in the USSR as it was owned and operated by the State. The beginnings of Soviet civil aviation at the inception of the Russian Soviet Federated Socialist Republic (RSFSR) were meager as the new Soviet government did not have an organization to regulate and supervise civil aviation in the newly formed republic.

On January 31, 1921, Lenin ordered the creation of an organization called The Chief Administration of the Civil Air Fleet which would organize the formation of civil aviation in the republic. By May 1921, experimental passenger service and mail flights were conducted using Ilya Muromets four-engine airplanes.

On February 3, 1923, the Sovnarkom (Council of Peoples Commissars) approved plans for a State owned and operated airline under the direction of the State's Red Air Fleet. It is this date which is officially accepted as the beginning of Soviet civil aviation. On March 17, 1923, the first Soviet airline named Dobrolet was formed.

After the formation of Dobrolet in the RSFSR, airlines in other regions of the USSR were created. In the Ukraine an airline named Ukrvozdukhput was formed and passenger and air cargo services were provided. On October 1923, representatives from the Soviet Republics in Central Asia held meetings with officials of Dobrolet in Moscow with proposals of forming a sub-division of Dobrolet based in Tashkent, Uzbekskaya SSR. This sub-division of Dobrolet would be responsible for aviation services in the whole of Soviet Central Asia. On September 21, 1926, Dobrolet became an All-Union airline instead of being exclusively Russian as its services ex-

60th Year of Aeroflot 1923-1983 Commemorative Table Medallion. **$80-$85**

panded throughout all areas of the USSR. In 1928, Dobrolet and Ukrvozdukhput were merged as Soviet civil aviation was being reorganized. On February 25, 1932, the Chief Directorate of the Civil Air Fleet took control of all Soviet civil aviation activities and the basic structure for the operation of air services within the USSR was established. It was on March 25, 1932, that Aeroflot became the official name of the Soviet airline.

In order to develop the Soviet economy, expansion of civil aviation in European Russia, Soviet Central Asia and Siberia was necessary. During the first Five-Year Plan (1928-1932), the Soviet government placed emphasis on creating a Soviet aircraft industry capable of manufacturing Soviet built aircraft for its civil aviation fleet. The most notable Soviet built aircraft of that period were the single-engine, eight passenger, Kalinin K-5 for domestic routes and the larger, three-engine, nine passenger Tupolev ANT-9 for international routes. The Polikarpov U-2 was a single-engine light biplane that could carry three passengers and cargo. Approximately 33,000 were built in many versions for short-haul operations within the

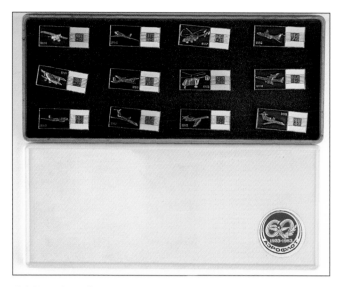

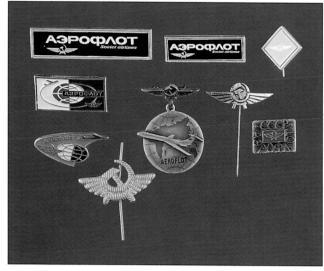

60th Year of Aeroflot 1923-1983 Commemorative Pin Set with box. **$55-$65**

Aeroflot Lapel Pins, c. 1970s-1980s. **$5-$10**

USSR. By the year 1930, fifty percent of the aircraft flown serving routes in the USSR were still foreign built.

During the second Five-Year Plan (1933-1937), it was decided that Soviet civil aviation would become one of the major modes of transportation linking the major cities within the USSR. In conjunction with this the Soviet aircraft industry would have to grow in size so that the Civil Air Fleet could become less dependent on foreign aircraft. During the third Five-Year Plan (1938-1942), a large-scale airport construction

programme was undertaken as improvements were made to airports throughout the USSR.

It was on June 22, 1941, that the German military invaded the Soviet Union. The Sovnarkom (Council of People's Commissars) directed the Chief Directorate of the Civil Air Fleet to mobilize the Civil Air Fleet in the war effort. Aeroflot became part of the Red Army Transport Command providing transport aircraft for supply missions, military personnel movement, evacuation and liaison duties. The Civil Air Fleet flew over 1.5

Right: Aeroflot Award Banner, c. 1983. **$75-$95**
Velvet, 22" x 14 1/4".
Text on front: Winner in a Socialist Competition in Honour of the 60th Year of Civil Aviation.

Aeroflot Award Banner, c. 1985. **$75-$95**
Velvet, 25 1/2" x 14 1/2".
Text on front: Leningrad Order of the October Revolution
Administration of Civil Aviation
Northern Territorial Committee of the Trade Unions
of Aviation Workers.
Text on back -
Slogan on top: "We Will Come to the Victory of Communist Labour!"
(V.I. Lenin)
Text on bottom: Winner in a Socialist Competition in Honour of the 40th Year of the Victory of the Soviet People in the Great Patriotic War 1941-1945.

million military related missions during the 'Great Patriotic War' (World War II). On the western front Aeroflot's main concern was in the war effort but in the regions of the USSR unaffected by the war Aeroflot continued with its civil aviation duties.

After the completion of the war, especially in the European region of the USSR, extensive repairs were required to airports, terminal buildings, maintenance hangars and air traffic control installations to restore the services provided by Aeroflot. During the fourth Five-Year Plan (1946-1950), the Soviet government concentrated its efforts on the development of Aeroflot services between Moscow and the capitals of the union republics and other major administrative and industrial centers. During the last year of the Plan 1950, Aeroflot carried more than 1.6 million passengers and carried over 180,000 tons of mail and cargo largely due to the success of the Ilyushin Il-12 which went into service in 1947.

During the fifth Five-Year Plan (1951-1955), all major airports restricted to daylight operations only had night flying equipment installed to improve the airport's utilization. Civil air transport grew rapidly in the early 1950s and the Chief Directorate of the Civil Air Fleet was placed under the control of the Soviet government's Council of Ministers. At the end of the fifth Five-Year Plan in 1955, Aeroflot carried 2.5 million passengers plus more than a quarter of a million tons of mail and freight. During this time period Aeroflot achieved these increases in volume using twin-engine propeller driven Li-2 and Il-12 aircraft which were also in use during the previous Five-Year Plan.

Before the 'Great Patriotic War' the Soviet Union acquired a number of Douglas DC-3's which were operated by Aeroflot. The Lisonov Li-2's were DC-3's built under license in the Soviet Union. The Soviet built Li-2's were powered by two 1,000 hp Shvetsov Ash-62IR air-cooled radial engines. The Li-2 carried twenty-one passengers and became the major aircraft in operation with Aeroflot immediately after the war. The Li-2 had a cruising speed of 155 mph with a maximum payload-range of 870 nautical miles. There were approximately 2,000 Li-2's built.

The other aircraft of major importance for Aeroflot after the war was the Soviet designed and built Ilyushin Il-12. It was a piston twin-engine, tricycle-gear airplane that could carry twenty-one passengers. The Il-12 had two 1,650 hp Shvetsov ASh-82FN fourteen-cylinder, air-cooled radial engines. By 1955, the Il-12's had replaced the Li-2's on international routes. The Il-12 had a cruising speed of 220 mph with a maximum

Left: Tupolev Tu-104 Pin. **$5-$10**

Right: Ilyushin Il-18 Pin. **$5-$10**

payload-range of 1000 nautical miles. Approximately 200 Il-12's were in operation with Aeroflot by the year 1950.

By the end of the sixth Five-Year Plan (1956-1960), Aeroflot's capacity was to double and its passenger traffic was to reach 16 million. Consideration had to be given to the large distances to be covered throughout the USSR. In order to achieve these goals modern high capacity turboprop and turbojet aircraft were to be introduced. The introduction of these new generation aircraft would be utilized on domestic trunk routes and international routes as well. Airports in the main cities of the USSR would also have to be modernized to accommodate these new aircraft.

The first jet airplane operated by Aeroflot was the Tupolev Tu-104. On September 15, 1956, the Tu-104 went into regular service. At that time the Tu-104 was the only jet aircraft in airline service in the world and it had the unique Soviet 'rustic' appearance. The Tu-104 twinjet had two 14,881 lbs. Mikulin AM-3 turbojets each mounted at the wing root. Some of the notable 'Tupolev' features of the airplane were the wing's marked anhedral and that the landing gear were stored in streamlined farings that were on the trailing edge of the wings outboard of the engines. The flight deck was unique for a civil airliner, as the two pilots were separated by a passageway to the navigator's compartment at a lower level in the extreme nose. The navigator compartment's nose was glazed, which was quite useful for visual flight over remote areas of the USSR. The nose of the Tu-104 was the same as that of the Tu-16 bomber which was the airplane from which it was derived. The original Tu-104 could carry fifty passengers at cruising speeds of up to 500 mph over a maximum payload-range of 1,430 nautical miles with one-hour fuel reserves. Between 200 to 250 Tu-104's were built for Aeroflot.

The next economic plan introduced by the Soviet government, deviating from the normal trend, was a Seven-Year Plan (1959-1965). Civil aviation would continue to see tremendous growth in the USSR. To facilitate this airports would continue to be modernized and Aeroflot would be supplied with more modern turbojet and turboprop aircraft. In 1959 the first year of the Plan, two new turboprop aircraft entered passenger service with Aeroflot.

On April 20, 1959, the Ilyushin Il-18 entered passenger service with Aeroflot. It was designed to fulfill Aeroflot's requirement for a high-capacity medium range turboprop that would be versatile enough to operate over the majority of its route system and be capable of operating from less sophisticated airports. It was a large low-wing, fully pressurized, four-engine turboprop aircraft. It was powered by four 4,000 hp Ivchenko AI-20 turboprops. In addition to its domestic routes, the Il-18's operated over many of Aeroflot's long-distance international routes including those to Africa and Asia. For many years the Il-18 was the most important airplane in the Aeroflot fleet as up to 650 were in operation with the airline. The Il-18 could carry eighty passengers at cruising speeds of up to 400 mph over a maximum payload-range of 1,350 nautical miles with one-hour fuel reserves.

On July 22, 1959, the Antonov An-10 entered passenger service with Aeroflot. It was a high-wing, four-engine turboprop, with landing gear designed for soft-field operations. It was designed for medium-haul routes with high passenger capacity and could operate from smaller aerodromes with unprepared strips. It had four 4,000 hp Ivchenko AI-20 turboprops. The An-10 could carry eighty-five passengers at cruising speeds of up to 410 mph over a maximum payload-range of 660 nautical miles with one-hour fuel reserves. More than 500 An-10s and its successor the An-12's were built for Aeroflot.

On April 24, 1961, the world's largest airliner entered into service with Aeroflot the Tupolev Tu-114. It was developed for Aeroflot's long-range requirements and was derived from the Tu-95 long-range bomber. The Tu-114 was a greatly modified version of the Soviet Air Force's Tu-95 as its wings were repositioned at the base of the newly designed fuselage and the tailplane was also lowered. As with the Tu-104, the airplane retained the navigator compartment with its glazed nose. Other notable 'Tupolev' features of the airplane were the wing's marked anhedral and that the landing gear were stored in streamlined farings that were on the trailing-edge of the wings aft of the inboard engines. It was a very large airplane powered by the largest turboprops ever, the 12,000 ehp Kuznetsov NK-12M engines driving 18 ft 4.5 in diameter, eight-blade counter-rotating propellers. It could carry 220 passengers at cruising speeds of up to 480 mph over a maximum payload-range of 3,345 nautical miles with one-hour fuel reserves. Aeroflot operated approximately 30 Tu-114's.

Left: Aviation USSR Tu-114 1957 Pin. **$5-$10**

Right: Antonov An-24 Pin. **$5-$10**

A year later in 1962, Aeroflot added two new additional modern aircraft the Tupolev Tu-124 twinjet and the Antonov An-24 turboprop.

The Tu-124 was powered by two 11,905 lbs. of thrust Soloviev D-20P turbofans. The Tu-124 was the first short-to-medium range passenger jet to be powered by turbofan engines as turbofan engines are more efficient than turbojet engines. The Tu-124 very much resembled the Tu-104 but was twenty-five percent smaller than its predecessor. The Tu-124 was designed to replace the piston-engine Il-14 and the Li-2 on low density, short-haul routes flying in and out of unprepared airstrips. Even though it was a jet aircraft it had to have excellent airfield performance to be able to operate from smaller airfields. To accomplish this the aircraft had a high-lift airfoil section with double-slotted flaps at the wing's trailing edge and it also had low-pressure tires. The original Tu-124 could carry forty-four passengers at cruising speeds up to 500 mph over a maximum payload-range of approximately 675 nautical miles with one-hour fuel reserves. Approximately 100 Tu-124's were in operation with Aeroflot.

The An-24 was a high wing, twin-engine turboprop with a capacity of forty-four passengers. It was designed for local and regional short and medium range routes, from small airfields, in various climates and airfield elevations. It was powered by two Ivchenko AI-24 turboprops delivering a take-off power of 2,550 ehp. It had a cruising speed of up to 310 mph and a maximum payload-range 350 nautical miles with one-hour fuel reserves. Approximately 150 An-24's were in operation with Aeroflot.

During the last year of the Seven-Year Plan in 1965, Aeroflot carried over 42 million passengers, an increase of approximately thirty million passengers from the yearly passenger loads at the beginning of the Seven-Year Plan. In addition, Aeroflot also carried over one-million tons of mail and cargo. This surge of passenger growth was a direct result of the abundance of modern turbojet and turboprop aircraft put into service.

During the eighth Five-Year Plan (1966-1970), the Soviet government wanted to almost double Aeroflot's annual passenger traffic to approximately seventy million. In order to achieve this, airports would have to be modernized with automated baggage handling facilities and computers would have to be utilized for seat reservations. Also more modern jet airliners would have to be put into service. During the period of this Five-Year Plan, Aeroflot carried a total of more than 302 million passengers and approximately 6,500 million tons of cargo plus more than 1,600 million tons of mail. By 1970, the last year of the Plan, Aeroflot was serving over 3,500 destinations within the USSR.

In 1967, two new aircraft entered service with Aeroflot the Tupolev Tu-134 and the Ilyushin Il-62. The Tupolev Tu-134 was designed to replace the Tu-124 in service with Aeroflot. The Tu-134 had an increased passenger capacity, two rear mounted engines, T-tail, and still had the capability to operate from small airfields with unprepared strips. The rear mounted engines had greater passenger appeal as the cabin noise was much quieter than the wing-root mounted engines of the Tu-124. Many of the 'Tupolev' design features still remained such as the navigator compartment's glazed nose, the wing's marked anhedral with wing-mounted landing gear pods, which aided in the stability of the aircraft while landing on unprepared runways. The Tu-134 started passenger service with Aeroflot in August 1967. It had two rear-mounted 14,991 lbs. of thrust Soloviev D-30 turbofans. The Tu-134 could carry seventy-two passengers at a cruising speed of up to 550 mph over a maximum payload-range of 1,295 nautical miles with one-hour fuel reserves. More than 200 were in service with Aeroflot.

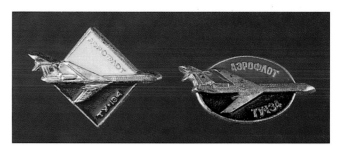

Tupolev Tu-134 Pins. **$5-$10**

Photograph of an Ilyushin Il-62 at Toronto's International Airport taken in the early 1970s.

1/100 Scale Model of the IL-62, c. 1980s.
This kit was manufactured by VEB Plasticart, East Germany.

The Ilyushin Il-62 was designed for Aeroflot's intercontinental routes and replaced the Tu-114 turboprops. The Il-62 was a handsome airplane with four rear mounted turbofan engines, a high T-tail with large bullet fairing at its top, a cockpit with eighteen windows and a large radome at its nose. The wings had a distinctive 'dog-tooth' aerodynamic feature at one-third the span of each wing's leading edge to enhance its low speed characteristics. The Il-62 was powered by four rear mounted 23,148 lbs. of thrust Kuznetsov Nk-8 turbofans. It entered passenger service with Aeroflot on September 15, 1967.

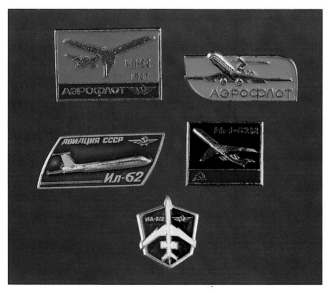

Ilyushin Il-62 Pins. **$5-$10**

It could carry 162 passengers at a cruising speed of up to 560 mph over a maximum payload-range of 3,615 nautical miles with one-hour fuel reserves. Aeroflot operated approximately 150 Il-62's.

During this eighth Five-Year Plan, another unique aircraft entered service with Aeroflot. In the late 1960s, 'Local Service' routes were still being flown with the aging piston-engine Il-12's and Li-2's. They were replaced by more modern jet and turboprop aircraft in the late 1950s on the 'All-Union Services' and international routes which they originally flew. It was decided to replace these antiquated Il-12's and Li-2's with a unique jet aircraft that would have greater passenger comfort, double the cruising speed, while having short take-off and landing capabilities and able to operate from unprepared strips. The result was the Yakovlev Yak-40, a unique aircraft in a class all its own.

The Yak-40 was a rear mounted tri-jet with an unswept low-wing and T-tail configuration. It was powered by three rear mounted 3,306 lbs. of thrust Ivchenko AI-25 turbofans which was unique for an aircraft of its size. Its three engines and unswept wing gave the jet excellent airfield performance characteristics. Aeroflot first flew the Yak-40 in passenger service on September 30, 1968. It could carry twenty-four passengers at a cruising speed of up to 340 mph over a maximum payload-range of 970 nautical miles with reserves. Approximately 1,000 Yak-40s were built for Aeroflot.

During the ninth Five-Year Plan (1971-1975), discussions were held on the continued increase in passenger traffic with Aeroflot. The Il-62 and Tu-134 jets were used on long-to-medium haul routes, while the An-24 turboprop and the Yak-40 jet were used on short-and-medium haul routes.

New aircraft to emerge during this ninth Five-Year Plan were the Tupolev Tu-154 tri-jet and the Tu-144 supersonic airliner (SST).

The Tupolev Tu-154 was designed as a replacement for the Tu-104, Il-18 and An-10 on medium-to-long haul routes. It entered passenger service with Aeroflot on February 9, 1972. The Tu-154 was a rear engine tri-jet with a T-tail. As with other Tupolev airliners, the Tu-154 had wings with a marked anhedral with wing-mounted landing gear pods. Each main landing gear bogie had a total of six tires (three pairs) to enable this large airplane to operate from unprepared runways. One Tupolev feature that was omitted however was the glazed nose which was replaced by a conventional radome. It was powered by three rear mounted 20,943 lbs. of thrust Kuznetsov NK-8-2 turbofans. It could carry 158 passengers at a cruising speed of

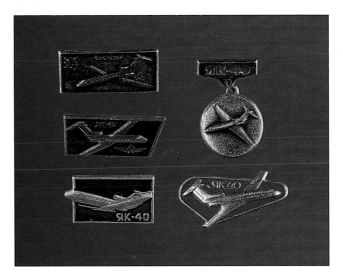
Yakovlev Yak-40 Pins. **$5-$10**

1/100 Scale Model of the Tu-154, c. 1980s.
This kit was manufactured by VEB Plasticart, East Germany.

Tupolev Tu-154 Pins. **$5-$10**

560 mph over a maximum payload-range of 1,540 nautical miles plus reserves. There were more than 300 Tu-154's in service with Aeroflot.

The Tupolev Tu-144 was the Soviet Union's supersonic transport (SST). On December 31, 1968, the Tu-144 became the world's first SST to fly. The prototype Tu-144 was a full-scale flying test-bed. At the Paris Air Show of June 1973, the production form of the Tu-144 was displayed and took part in the air show. It was a substantially modified version of the original prototype. The Tu-144 was an elegant looking airplane. Added to the production variant were two canards at the top of the fuselage just aft of the flight deck. They were normally extended during take-off and landing to improve low-speed handling and were retracted during cruise flight. The Tu-144 looked like a graceful pre-historic bird when flying at low airspeeds with the canards extended and the nose-visor in the lowered position. It was powered by four 28,660 lbs. of thrust Kuznetsov NK-144 turbofan engines mounted beneath its double-delta wing plan form. It could carry up to 140 passengers at Mach 2.2 for a maximum payload-range of 3,500 nautical miles.

Unfortunately at the June Paris Air Show the Tu-144 on display crashed during its flight demonstration. The actual cause of the crash is still unknown though pilot error is a possible cause. By December 26, 1975, the Tu-144 was flying on regularly scheduled supersonic flights carrying freight and mail. Scheduled passenger flights with Aeroflot began on November 1, 1977. After 102 flights services were canceled as an accident occurred in flight. The Tu-144 was plagued with engine fuel control and other technical problems and as a result the Tu-144 was removed from service with Aeroflot.

During the tenth Five-Year Plan (1976-1980), the Soviets were planning the introduction of a large wide-body aircraft to meet its domestic and international route requirements. The resultant aircraft built was the Ilyushin Il-86.

The Ilyushin Il-86 was a large wide-body, four engine, low-wing aircraft. The Il-86 was a unique aircraft having a double-deck fuselage. In the lower deck, the passengers would board the aircraft via three air-stair doors which reached ground level and put their baggage away in the cargo compartments. Then via three internal staircases they would climb to the upper main passenger cabin and find their seats. This innovation allowed Aeroflot to operate this large 350 passenger aircraft to airports throughout the USSR that did not have the facilities to handle such a large aircraft. The Il-86 was powered by four 28,660 lbs. of thrust Kuznetsov NK-86 turbofan engines. It

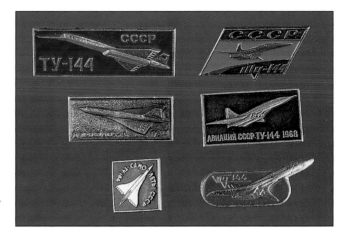

Tupolev Tu-144 Supersonic Transport (SST) Pins. **$5-$10**

Ilyushin Il-86 Pin. **$5-$10**

Antonov An-26 Transport Aircraft Pin. **$5-$10**

Large Heavy-Lift Transports of the Soviet Airline Aeroflot Pin Set.
1. Il-86 **$5-$10**
2. An-124 **$5-$10**
3. Mi-26 **$5-$10**

had a cruising speed of up to 590 mph over a maximum-payload range of 2,000 nautical miles. The Il-86 was introduced on routes with Aeroflot in 1978.

In addition to providing passenger services, Aeroflot also provided other services for the Soviet economy in many different forms. It provided cargo services, air ambulance, agricultural spraying, forest patrol, fire fighting, fish spotting, prospecting and construction. A variety of aircraft were used to provide these services, An-12, An-26, An-22, An-124, and Il-76 cargo aircraft. In addition to the fixed-wing aircraft, Ka-26,

Mi-4, Mi-6, Mi-8, Mi-10K, and Mi-26 helicopters were used in applications were a helicopter would be best suited. Aeroflot's fleet of aircraft were always ready to be put to use for the Soviet military if it was required by the State.

Aeroflot was State owned and operated and was the only airline in the USSR. It was the largest airline in the world and operated routes covering approximately 693,000 miles in length. Seventy-eight percent of the routes were domestic and twenty-two percent of the routes were international. The airline carried annually more than 120,000,000 passengers. Aeroflot, the Soviet Airlines, ceased to exist with the collapse of the Soviet Union in December 1991. It was divided into separate airlines of the Confederation of Independent States (CIS).

Ilyushin Il-76 Pin. $5-$10

Aeroflot Excellence Award Badge, c. 1940s-1960s. $65-$85

Antonov An-124 Pin. $5-$10

Mil Mi-4 Civil Aviation Helicopter Pin. $5-$10

Left: Aeroflot (Civil Air Fleet) 500,000 Km. Safe Flight Award Badge, c. 1950s-1960s. $45-$55

Right: Aeroflot (Civil Air Fleet) 1,000,000 Km. Safe Flight Award Badge, c. 1950s-1960s. $65-$85

Aeroflot for Safe Flight 5000 Hours Pilot Award Badge, c. 1950s-1960s. $45-$55

Right: Aeroflot Pilot's Peaked Hat Cap Badge with Wing Badge on Crown, c. 1970s-1980s. $10-$15

185

Aeroflot Academy Graduation Badge. **$45-$55**

Moscow Institute for the Aviation Industry Academy Graduation Badge, c. 1950s-1960s. **$45-$55**

Leningrad Institute for the Aviation Industry Academy Graduation Badge, c. 1970s-1980s. **$35-$45**

Ministry of Aviation Lapel Pin. **$10-$15**

Right: Public Inspector for the Safety of Flight Badge, c. 1970s-1980s. **$25-$35**

Aeroflot Award Banner, c. 1984. **$75-$95**
Velvet, 25 1/2" x 14 1/2".
Text on front: Leningrad Administration of Civil Aviation
Northern Territorial Committee of the Trade Unions of Aviation Workers.
Text on back -
Slogan on top: "We Will Come to the Victory of Communist Labour!" (V.I. Lenin)
Text on bottom: Winner in a Socialist Competition in Honour of the 50th Year of the Leningrad Administration of Civil Aviation 1984.

50th Year of the Ilyushin Design Bureau Medal. **$45-$55**
Text on back: OKB (Experimental Construction (Design) Bureau) in the name of S.V. Ilyushin 1933-1983.

Tupolev Design Bureau Honourary Veteran Badge, c. 1970s. **$25-$45**
Text on front: Aviation Scientific-Technical Complex in the Name of A.N. Tupolev.

Aeroflot 100th Anniversary of Lenin's Birth 1970 Commemorative Pin, c.1970. **$5-$10**

Aeroflot Flight Over the Equator Pins, c. 1970s-1980s. **$5-$10**

Left: Air Fleets of the USSR Commemorative Pin, c. 1970s-1980s. **$5-$10**

Right: Aeroflot 'Good Travel' Pin, c. 1970s-1980s. **$5-$10**

Aeroflot Airliner Pin Set, c. 1970s-1980s. **$5-$10 each**
1. Tu-134
2. Il-62M
3. Tu-154

Aeroflot Airliner Pin Set, c. 1960s. **$5-$10 each**
1. Il-18
2. Tu-114
3. Il-62
4. Tu-144

Aeroflot Airliner Pin Set, c. 1970s-1980s.
$5-$10 each
1. Tu-134
2. Il-62
3. Tu-154
4. Il-76

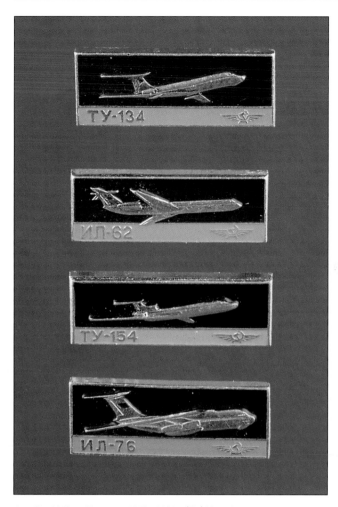

Aeroflot Airliner Pin set, c. 1970s-1980s. **$5-$10 each**
1. Tu-134
2. Il-62
3. Tu-154
4. Il-76

Aeroflot Airliner Pin Set, c. 1960s. **$5-$10 each**
1. Il-12
2. Tu-114
3. An-22
4. Il-62
5. Tu-154

BIBLIOGRAPHY

Andrew, Christopher & Gordievsky, Oleg. *KGB – The Inside Story*. London: Hodder & Stoughton, 1990.

Averyanov, A. K. & Amelin, A. A. & Krivoshein, O. C. & Nazarov, I. N. *Vladimir Ilyich Lenin – Life and Work*. Moscow: Progress Publishers, 1985.

Barron, John. *MiG Pilot – The Final Escape of Lieutenant Belenko*. New York: Reader's Digest Association, Inc., 1980.

Bonds, Ray. *Russian Military Power*. New York: Bonanza Books, 1982.

Borisov, V.A. *The Badges of Soviet Armed Forces*. St. Peterburg: Farn, 1994.

Brown, Archie & Kaser, Michael & Smith, Gerald. *The Cambridge Encyclopedia of Russia and the Former Soviet Union*. London: Press Syndicate of the Cambridge University, 1994.

Butowski, Piotr & Miller, Jay. *OKB – MiG, A History of the Design Bureau and Its Aircraft*. England: Specialty Press Publishers and Wholesalers, Inc., 1991.

Clark, Ronald W. *Lenin – A Biography*. New York: Harper & Row Publishers, 1988.

Dmytryshyn, Basil. *A Concise History – USSR*. New York: Charles Scribner's Sons, 1965.

Dornberg, John. *Brezhnev – The Masks of Power*. New York: Basic Books, Inc., 1974.

Editors Time – Life Books. *The Soviet Union*. Amsterdam: Time – Life Books, 1984.

Energia. S.P. Korolev *Space Corporation Energia – From First Satellite to Energia*. Moscow: Energia, 1994.

Fischer, Louis. *The Life of Lenin*. New York: Harper & Row Publishers, 1964.

Furlan, M. *USSR Decorations Orders and Medals*. Toronto: Militaria House, 1988.

Furlan, M. *Soviet Army Insignia. 1917-1985*. Toronto: Militaria House, 1990.

Gatland, Kenneth. *The Pocket Encyclopedia of Spaceflight in Colour – Manned Spacecraft*. London: Blandford Press, 1967.

Glushko, V.P. *USSR Academy of Sciences – Rocket Engines GDL-OKB*. Moscow: Novosti Press Agency Publishing House, 1975.

Gorbachev, Mikhail. *The August Coup*. New York: Harper Collins Publishers, 1991.

Green, William & Swanborough, Gordon. *The Observer's Soviet Aircraft Directory*. London: Frederwick Warne & Co. Ltd., 1975.

Gromyko, Andrei. *Memories*. London: Hutchinson, 1989.

Gunston, Bill. *The Illustrated Encyclopedia of Commercial Aircraft*. London: Phoebus Publishing Company, 1980.

Gunston, Bill. *The Illustrated Encyclopedia of Propeller Airliners*. London: Phoebus Publishing Company, 1980.

Gunston, Bill. *Modern Soviet Air Force*. New York: Arco Publishing, Inc., 1982.

Gunston, Bill. *Aircraft of the Soviet Union – The Encyclopedia of Soviet Aircraft Since 1917*. London: Osprey Publishing, 1983.

Gunston, Bill. *Mikoyan MiG-21*. London: Osprey Publishing House Limited, 1986.

Hamlyn, Paul. *The Encyclopedia of Space*. Paris: Hamlyn Publishing Group Ltd., 1967.

Hart, Douglas. *The Encyclopedia of Soviet Spacecraft*. London: Bison Books Ltd., 1987.

Heller, Mikhail & Nekrich, Aleksander M. *Utopia In Power*. New York: Summit Books, 1986.

Huges, Gwyneth & Welfare, Simon. *Red Empire – The Forbidden History of the USSR*. London: Weidenfeld and Nicolson, 1990.

Hyde, H. Montgomery. *Stalin – The History of a Dictator*. New York: Harford Productions, 1971.

Ilyinskii, V. N. *Heroism – Labour Glory*. Moscow: Publisher of Political Literature, 1987.

Johnson, Nicholas L. *Handbook of Soviet Space Flight*. California: Univelt Inc., 1980.

Johnson, Nicholas L. *Soviet Space Programmes 1980-1985*. California: Univelt Inc., 1987.

Johnson, Nicholas L. *The Soviet Reach for the Moon*. USA: Cosmos Books, 1994.

Jordon, John. *Modern Soviet Navy*. New York: Arco Publishing, Inc., 1982.

Khrushchev, Nikita. *The Last Testament*. Boston: Little, Brown and Company (Inc.), 1974.

Kibalchich, O. *XXVI Congress – The Future of the USSR's Economic Regions*. Moscow: Progress Publishers, 1981.

King, David. *Trotsky – A Photographic Biography*. Oxford: Basil Blackwell Ltd., 1986.

Koenig, William & Scofield, Peter. *Soviet Military Power*. Greenwich, CT: Bison Books Corporation, 1983.

Korkeshkin, A. *The Soviet Armed Forces – Questions and Answers*. Moscow: Novosti Press Agency Publishing House, 1975.

Krivtsov, V.D. *Avers No.2 – Soviet Badges and Jetons – Catalogue for Collectors*. Moscow: Avers, 1996.

Kutsenko, A. N. & Pudichenko, A. I. *Symbols of Excellence of the Law Enforcement Organizations*. Kiev: Donetsk, 1991.

Lichitskii, I. I. *The Art of Russian Metal Miniatures – Catalogue of Award Badges*. Lvov: S.P. "Udacha", 1995.

MacDonald, Hugh. *Aeroflot – Soviet Air Transport Since 1923*. London: Putnam, 1975.

Marrin, Albert. *Stalin – Russia's Man of Steel*. New York: Viking Kestrel, 1988.

Marx, K. & Engels. F. *Manifesto of the Communist Party*. Moscow: Progress Publishers, 1969.

Matson, Dr. Wayne R. *Cosmonautics – A Colorful History*. Washington D.C.: Cosmos Books, 1994.

McDaniel, Paul & Schmitt, Paul J. *The Comprehensive Guide to Soviet Orders and Medals*. Arlington, Va.: Historical Research, 1997.

Mondey, David. *Encyclopedia of the World's Commercial and Private Aircraft*. New York: Crescent Books, 1981.

Mondey, David. *The Encyclopedia of Major Airliners of the World*. London: Temple Press Aerospace Publishing, 1983.

Moon, Howard. *Soviet SST The Techno-Politics of the Tu-144*. New York: Orion Books, 1989.

Moore, Captain John E. *Warships of the Soviet Navy*. London: Jane's Publishing Company Limited, 1981.

Moynahan, Brian. *The Russian Century – A Photographic History of Russia's 100 Years*. New York: Random House, 1994.

Nemecek, Vaclav. *The History of Soviet Aircraft from 1918*. Great Britain: Key Publishing Ltd., 1986.

Nenarokov, Albert Pavlovich. *An Illustrated History of the Great October Socialist Revolution-1917 Month by Month*. Moscow: Progress Publishers, 1987.

Novosti. *Salyut Orbiting Stations*. Moscow: The Novosti Press Agency Publishing House, 1975.

Novosti Press. *Transfer In Orbit*. Moscow: Novosti Press, 1969.

Payne, Robert. *The Life and Death of Lenin*. New York: Simon and Schuster, 1964.

Payne, Robert. *The Life and Death of Trotsky*. New York: McGraw-Hill Book Co., 1977.

Petrovich, Professor G.V. *The Soviet Encyclopedia of Space Flight*. Moscow: Mir Publishers, 1969.

Pipes, Richard. *The Russian Revolution*. New York: Alfred A. Knopf, 1990.

Pipes, Richard. *A Concise History of the Russian Revolution*. New York: Alfred A. Knopf, 1995.

Putnikov, Georgi. *Orders and Medals of the USSR*. Moscow: Novosti, 1990.

Radzinsky, Edvard. *Stalin – The First In-Depth Biography Based on Explosive New Documents from Russia's Secret Archives*. New York: Doubleday, 1996.

Raibchikov, Evgeny. *Russians in Space*. New York: Doubleday, 1971.

Reed, John. *Ten Days that Shook the World*. Moscow: Progress Publishers, 1987.

Robinson, Anthony. *Soviet Air Power*. London: Bison Books Ltd., 1985.

Romanov, A. *Spacecraft Designer – The Story of Sergei Korolev*. Moscow: Novosti Press Agency Publishing House, 1976.

Sakwa, Richard. *Soviet Politics – An Introduction*. London: Routledge, 1989.

Schlesinger Jr., Arthur M. *Stalin – World Leaders Past & Present*. New York: Chelsea House Publishers, 1985.

Schlesinger Jr., Arthur M. *Khrushchev – World Leaders Past & Present*. New York: Chelsea House Publishers, 1986.

Shapiro, Leonard. *The Russian Revolutions of 1917- The Origins of Modern Communism*. New York: Basic Books, Inc., 1984.

Shefov, A. N. *Leniniana – In Soviet Discriptive Art*. Leningrad: "Iskusstvo" Leningrad Division, 1986.

Smith W. H. *Russia's Top Guns – Soviet Air Power*. New York: W. H. Smith Publishers, Inc., 1990.

Solovyov, Vladimir & Klepikova, Elena. *Boris Yeltsin – A Political Biography*. New York: G. P. Putnam's Sons, 1992.

Stroud, John. *Soviet Air Transport Since 1945*. England: Funk & Wagnall's, 1968.

Sweetman, Bill & Gunston, Bill. *Soviet Air Power – An Illustrated Encyclopedia of the Warsaw Pact Air Forces Today*. London: Salamander Books Limited, 1978.

Sweetman, Bill. *The Presidio Concise Guide to Soviet Military Aircraft*. California: Precidio Press, 1981.

Sweetman, Bill. *Modern Fighting Aircraft – MiG's*. New York: Arco Publishing, 1985.

Taylor, John W. R. *Jane's All the World's Aircraft*. England: Jane's Publishing Company Limited, 1968, 1974, 1984.

Taylor, John W. R. *Aircraft, Strategy and Operations of the Soviet Air Force*. London: Jane's Publishing Company Limited, 1986.

Trotsky, Leon. *History of the Russian Revolution*. New York: Pathfinder, 1998.

Ulam, Adam B. *Stalin – The Man and His Era*. Boston: Beacon Press, 1973.

Vail, John J. *"Peace, Land, Bread!" - A History of the Russian Revolution*. New York: Facts On File, Inc., 1996.

Vazhin, F. *The Soviet Air Force*. Moscow: Novosti Press Agency Publishing House, 1975.

Volkogonov, Dmitri. *Trotsky – The Eternal Revolutionary*. London: The Free Press, 1992.

Volkogonov, Dmiri. *Lenin – A New Biography*. London: The Free Press, 1994.

Volkogonov, Dmitri. *Stalin – Triumph and Tragedy*. London: The Free Press, 1996.

Volkogonov, Dmitri, *Autopsy for an Empire – The Seven Leaders Who Built the Soviet Regime*. New York: Free Press, 1998.

Volkov-Lannit, L. F. *V. I. Lenin in Photographs*. Moscow: Publishers "Iskusstvo", 1969.

Weber, Gerda & Herman. *Lenin – Life and Works*. New York: Facts On File, Inc., 1980.

Zaloga, Steven J. Slava. *Udeloy and Sovremenniy*. Hong Kong: Concord Publications Company, 1992.

Zazersky, Yevgeni. *As the People Willed – A Documented Account of How the Union of Soviet Socialist Republics was Formed (1917-1922)*. Moscow: Novosti Press Agency Publishing House, 1972.